T0192627

Lean Software Systems Engineering for Developers

Managing Requirements, Complexity, Teams, and Change Like a Champ

Doug Durham
Chad Michel

Apress®

Lean Software Systems Engineering for Developers: Managing Requirements, Complexity, Teams, and Change Like a Champ

Doug Durham
Lincoln, NE, USA

Chad Michel
Lincoln, NE, USA

ISBN-13 (pbk): 978-1-4842-6932-9
https://doi.org/10.1007/978-1-4842-6933-6

ISBN-13 (electronic): 978-1-4842-6933-6

Copyright © 2021 by Doug Durham and Chad Michel

This work is subject to copyright. All rights are reserved by the Publisher, whether the whole or part of the material is concerned, specifically the rights of translation, reprinting, reuse of illustrations, recitation, broadcasting, reproduction on microfilms or in any other physical way, and transmission or information storage and retrieval, electronic adaptation, computer software, or by similar or dissimilar methodology now known or hereafter developed.

Trademarked names, logos, and images may appear in this book. Rather than use a trademark symbol with every occurrence of a trademarked name, logo, or image we use the names, logos, and images only in an editorial fashion and to the benefit of the trademark owner, with no intention of infringement of the trademark.

The use in this publication of trade names, trademarks, service marks, and similar terms, even if they are not identified as such, is not to be taken as an expression of opinion as to whether or not they are subject to proprietary rights.

While the advice and information in this book are believed to be true and accurate at the date of publication, neither the authors nor the editors nor the publisher can accept any legal responsibility for any errors or omissions that may be made. The publisher makes no warranty, express or implied, with respect to the material contained herein.

Managing Director, Apress Media LLC: Welmoed Spahr
Acquisitions Editor: Joan Murray
Development Editor: Laura Berendson
Coordinating Editor: Jill Balzano

Cover image designed by Freepik (www.freepik.com)

Distributed to the book trade worldwide by Springer Science+Business Media LLC, 1 New York Plaza, Suite 4600, New York, NY 10004. Phone 1-800-SPRINGER, fax (201) 348-4505, e-mail orders-ny@springer-sbm.com, or visit www.springeronline.com. Apress Media, LLC is a California LLC and the sole member (owner) is Springer Science + Business Media Finance Inc (SSBM Finance Inc). SSBM Finance Inc is a Delaware corporation.

For information on translations, please e-mail booktranslations@springernature.com; for reprint, paperback, or audio rights, please e-mail bookpermissions@springernature.com.

Apress titles may be purchased in bulk for academic, corporate, or promotional use. eBook versions and licenses are also available for most titles. For more information, reference our Print and eBook Bulk Sales web page at http://www.apress.com/bulk-sales.

Any source code or other supplementary material referenced by the author in this book is available to readers on GitHub via the book's product page, located at www.apress.com/9781484269329. For more detailed information, please visit http://www.apress.com/source-code.

Printed on acid-free paper

To my wife, Shana, who continually encourages me and fills my life with love, laughter, and happiness, and my father, Howard Durham, who showed me the importance of doing things the right way.

—Doug

To my wife Lisa, my son Sam, and my daughter Eva for all the support and encouragement during this endeavor.

—Chad

Table of Contents

About the Authors

Doug Durham is Co-founder and CEO of Don't Panic Labs, a firm that helps companies innovate through the design and development of software technologies. He is also the Co-founder of Nebraska Global, Don't Panic Lab's parent company, known as a pioneer in the startup landscape in Nebraska. Doug has more than three decades of software engineering and development experience in aerospace and defense, healthcare, manufacturing, ecommerce, consumer web applications, and Internet network services. He is passionate about the process of solving problems through software and the application of sound engineering principles and patterns to these efforts. His diverse skills, education, and various leadership roles have shaped his career. Doug served as a civil engineer in the Air National Guard for 21 years, which deployed him to many strange and wonderful places around the world before he retired at the rank of Major in 2006. Doug is a proud Husker and has an electrical engineering degree from the University of Nebraska-Lincoln, where all three of his children pursued STEM degrees. He has taught at the UNL Raikes School of Computer Science and serves on a College of Engineering advisory board. He also has a master's degree in finance and management. Doug often speaks at industry conferences on the topic of software engineering. He is a frequent guest lecturer at the University of Nebraska-Lincoln.

Chad Michel is Lead Software Architect for Don't Panic Labs with more than 20 years of software development and engineering experience. He holds a bachelor's degree in computer engineering and a master's degree in computer science. At Don't Panic Labs he works with clients to solve problems through innovative software solutions. Chad has worked for several companies in Lincoln, helping build a practice management application for lawyers, developing key features for an ecommerce application, and wrangling an Internet content delivery system into a stable platform. He regularly speaks at technical meetups hosted by Don't Panic Labs with significant contributions to the company blog. He also enjoys contributing at technical conferences and groups. Chad is a fourth-degree black belt in taekwondo.

About the Technical Reviewer

Jim Kudirka is the Founder and Principal Architect of Premier Software Systems, a company leading the change toward sustainable and repeatable best practices in software engineering. Through both practice and training, he has achieved mastery of the software development process and now dedicates his time to mentoring and coaching organizations.

Jim has nearly 28 years of software engineering experience, with 20 years leading development teams and projects to completion. He is passionate about good software design techniques and applying sound engineering principles that result in reduced time to market, exceptional quality, and minimizing overall cost.

Jim is a native Nebraskan, has a wife and two children, and received an electrical engineering degree from the University of Nebraska-Lincoln.

Acknowledgments

This book would not have happened if our co-workers, Bill Udell and Brian Zimmer, had not continually pushed us after we jokingly mentioned we should write a book. Bill and Brian were instrumental in connecting us with Joan Murray from Apress.

There were several people who helped bring this book together. First, Russ Guill and Shana Durham spent seemingly endless hours reviewing and revising our drafts. Sophie Lorenz and Jenna Buckley helped us with the development of some key graphics. Brian Zimmer and Andy Unterseher provided critical feedback on the content. Jim Kudirka provided a technical review of the book. We'd also like to thank the Apress team of Joan Murray, Laura Berendson, and Jill Balzano who helped guide and coach us through this process.

In 2010, Chad and I attended a Microsoft TechEd conference in New Orleans where we saw a presentation from Juval Löwy titled "The Zen of Architecture." This experience profoundly impacted my journey by connecting my previous background in systems engineering with how software should be engineered. Juval has become a de facto mentor for me and our company ever since. We are grateful for his insight into software engineering and his willingness to write a foreword for this book.

Special thanks to Steve Kiene and the whole Don't Panic Labs crew for enabling us to create a special company that has become an incredible laboratory for experimenting with and refining lean software systems engineering practices, processes, and methods. It is a joy to work with these wonderful people, and we feel lucky every day to do what we do.

Finally, we are grateful to our families for keeping us energized and curious and showing us that life is about collecting experiences.

Foreword

In life, good systems are better than goals. Regardless of how dire things are, it is better to have a system that allows you to keep improving and eventually attain your goals than it is to have obtained such goals but without any way of sustaining such success. I would argue that good systems are behind every success story you have ever heard about, be it of an individual, a company, or a product. Examples for the principle that good systems are better than goals are at every scope and task. For example, most people can get on a diet and lose some weight. At the same time, most people regain the weight (and then some) when they go off that diet. The key to permanently losing weight is to change your lifestyle, preferences, daily routine, diet, and even thinking process. In short, obtaining a better system. Which new developer would you rather hire? An experienced developer that knows the specifics of the technology at hand but is argumentative, avoids learning any new technology, and practices what that developer is already good at; or a developer that has little experience and does not know the current technology, but has a great can-do attitude, is eager to learn new technologies, to help teammates, and who cares deeply about quality? The reason you prefer the second developer is because that developer has a better system. It is even better to have a development process that reduces complexity and rework with good design, a process that accommodates quality control activities, and has zero tolerance for defects once found than it is to have a target of zero defects.

Perhaps the most extreme case of systems vs. goals is the upstarting Japanese automobile manufacturers and the established US automobile manufacturers in the years after the Second World War. In 1945, after several years of strategic bombing, Japan had no currency, no roads, no bridges, no power stations, no telephone lines, no factories, no cities, and no men. At the same time, the United States was the only advanced economy that survived the war unscathed. At the time when the Germans lived in rubbles and the British rationed food, the Americans were at the top of the world with their industrial and agricultural base operating at full capacity, with the reserve currency of the world, and millions of people ready to get back to work.

In 1947 Edward Deming (having given up on trying his techniques in the United States that was resting on its laurels) moved to Japan and started sharing his ideas on all aspects of manufacturing such as quality control, process, design, feedback loops, management, organization, and supply chains.

By the early 1950s, Toyota and Honda started adopting Deming's system and evolved it into what we now call just-in-time lean manufacturing. They transitioned from actual manufacturing into a process of continuous integration of ready-made components into any conceivable car. This enabled much better market segmentation due to the customization of the products. In fact, this was a level of variance that was unheard of, while maintaining a very fast response time to changes in the market. The new system did require a new grade of workers who were generalized specialists and could perform any of the tasks on the factory floor as the need arose. The system required the workers to own the process, to be familiar with every aspect of the factory, to collaborate in daily stand-up meetings on the objectives, to monitor the burndown rate of components, and to divide the work using the Kanban board. The new system eliminated inventory cost at both ends, at the factory and at the dealers, which in turn drastically reduced the final price. The most important aspect of Deming's idea was total quality management, where any worker was a quality vigilante, watching the process like a hawk with a relentless commitment for eliminating defects. The result was the best cars, at the best price, with the most customization. At the same time, this feat of engineering did require composable design of the assembly line to be able to assemble any car while not designing against any car in particular, flawless design of every artifact in the car, especially designing the components for reuse, and accurate calculations of the cost and schedule of every element (this process inspired Agile development).

By the 1960s the Japanese carmakers started dominating the US market, while the American car manufacturers stuck to their old systems. By the 1970s, the American car industry was finished.

Software development is nothing more than manufacturing code. This manufacturing should be impeccable as far as quality, must easily respond to changes, be done in the fastest possible way, at the lowest cost, and avoid unmitigated risks.

The only way to achieve these goals, be it at the individual, team, or company level, is to embrace a superior system. Even with minimal investment in architecture and project design, you can eliminate most of the rework and assign people in the most efficient way. Ideally, you should invest in a process that minimizes the potential for defects, as opposed to investing in debugging. All of that requires you to be proactive rather than reactive, something that is often more difficult to drive.

In this book, Doug Durham and Chad Michel outline their system for success in software development. Having this level of detailed prescription goes a long way toward demystifying the specific steps involved in setting up a better system. Part of it involves handling new technologies and technical leadership. However, most of the issues software development teams face today are not technical. Hardly any project fails because there was no good technical solution or a stronger language. To succeed, your team must deal with the soft issues of leadership, mentoring, communication, conflict resolution, as well as time management. You must design a system that allows developers to take pride in the quality of their work and their trade while avoiding classic mistakes. In this book, the authors share in a structured way their decades-long experience of how to install a good system.

Finally, I encourage you to develop your own good system motivated by this book. Adapt your system intelligently to your current environment. Devise an improvement plan to get there from where you are now. Learn new techniques, practice and tune them, maintain a curious mindset, keep improving, and always drive toward sustainable success even after you have moved to your next successful project.

—Juval Löwy
Founder and Architect
IDesign

Introduction

My main conclusion... is that software is hard. It's harder than anything else I've ever had to do.

—Donald Knuth Recipient of the 1974 ACM Turing Award[1]

If builders built houses the way programmers built programs, the first woodpecker to come along would destroy civilization.

—Gerald Weinberg[2]

One need only look at the rapid turnover in the companies making up the S&P 500 for evidence we are living in times of rapid change, innovation, and disruption. Whether you are a small software company or a large enterprise, your ability to be successful is directly related to your development teams' ability to rapidly respond to change. The responsibility of our software development teams is to enable this business agility. Our ability to do this will play a significant role in the success of our organization.

Making this task more challenging is the fact that everything about the problems we are trying to solve today is becoming more and more complex – the requirements, the solution, the hosting, the support, the pace of change, etc.

In March of 2021, we watched as NASA's Jet Propulsion Laboratory (JPL) successfully landed their latest Mars rover, Perseverance.[3] It is the second time they have successfully landed a vehicle, roughly the size and weight of a car (10-feet long, 9-feet wide, and weighing over 2200 lbs), using a complex, multistage landing sequence that concludes with a final stage that gently lowers the vehicle to the surface using something they call a sky crane. This entire landing process is fully automated which means software plays a large role in the process. It is another example of the amazing things we can achieve with software.

---

[1] *Knuth, Donald (2002). "All Questions Answered" (PDF). Notices of the AMS 49 (3): 320.*
[2] Weinberg attributed with the quote in: Murali Chemuturi (2010) *Mastering Software Quality Assurance: Best Practices, Tools and Technique for Software Developers.* p. ix.
[3] https://mars.nasa.gov/mars2020/

There is an enormous amount of complexity in landing a "car" on the surface of Mars. NASA's level of success is a result of their staff of scientists and engineers at JPL leaving nothing to chance. They manage this complexity by managing every aspect of the entire program. They understand that when details and decisions are left to chance, then outcomes can be negatively impacted.

The same is true when managing the complexity of any modern software system. Lack of structure and poor attention to detail result in increased errors in judgment and poor quality. These problems accumulate over time to create the software entropy or rot that we have all experienced. It is simply not enough to adopt agile methods or cherry-pick tools. We must look at the entire spectrum of the software development process, and ensure we leave nothing to chance. Anything less adds risk to our projects.

It is time our industry recognizes that we must approach software development as an engineering discipline to effectively manage both requirements and solution complexity. Those companies that make this transition will survive and flourish, but those that don't adapt will become less relevant. This is the difference between becoming a professional software engineer or remaining a programmer.

We have spent the last 15 years discovering how to integrate lean/agile practices within an engineering discipline that reduces errors in judgment and provides predictable outcomes, while still maintaining a high degree of agility and the ability to respond to change. Over the last ten years, our small team completed dozens of successful greenfield projects and product re-inventions. This allowed us to learn rapidly and refined our comprehensive approach that integrates best practices and modern techniques. This book provides the reader with an in-depth view into what we learned and how we approached this challenge.

The goal of this book is to provide the tools, references, and examples to allow software development teams of all skill levels to create the predictable, successful outcomes that enable them to manage the complexity of modern software system development and provide the agility their businesses need.

Why We Wrote This Book

While the body of knowledge around best practices and patterns has matured over the last four decades, many companies and software development teams continue to struggle with adopting these best practices and patterns within their organizations.

This has led to continued struggles to create and maintain software systems that provide the reliability, supportability, and extensibility required to effectively address the ever-increasing complexity of problems we need to solve via software.

We feel there are several reasons that contribute to this challenge. First, while many developers are familiar with the concepts that are considered best practices, many of them have had no first-hand experience with being part of a team that has successfully adopted them.

Second, many of the techniques, patterns, and practices have previously been presented by industry thought leaders. But they were presented in ways that make it difficult for developers of all skill levels to confidently advocate for them with management and implement them with a high degree of success. In addition, many of these sources are addressing only one portion of the problem, leaving the reader with an incomplete picture.

Third, the current university curriculum for training software developers continues to lack sufficient commitment to ensuring graduates have the necessary depth of understanding and experience to bring these patterns and practices to the industry. In our experience, teams that have adopted these best practices and patterns have relied on one or more individuals who took an interest in developing this understanding on their own, and had the capability to effectively advocate and ensure the successful adoption within their work environment. The problem is that these people tend to be unicorns.

Who This Book Is For

This book is for software developers and team leaders who have struggled to implement design and development best practices due to a lack of in-depth knowledge or experience. It's designed to provide the confidence and foundational skills needed to achieve success.

How This Book Is Organized

This book is divided into two parts. The first part, containing Chapters 1–6, outlines the motivation for focusing on targeted outcomes of development and then discusses these outcomes and how to achieve them. The second part, Chapters 7–8, covers the leadership required and planning considerations to achieve these desired outcomes. The following is a brief summary of the chapters.

Chapter 1: Focusing on Software Development Outcomes Instead of Outputs

Chapter 1 is dedicated to establishing the importance of focusing on desired outcomes as the goal of our engineering patterns and processes. It covers what it means to be a software engineer and highlights the core reasons for failures in our development processes: errors in judgment.

Chapter 2: Gaining a Shared Understanding Throughout the Project

Chapter 2 demonstrates how much risk and uncertainty is hidden because of our inability to establish a shared understanding of requirements and expectations. We provide guidance, tools, and examples for how to increase the level of shared understanding between stakeholders and members of the development team.

Chapter 3: Validation of User Experience

Chapter 3 discusses the nature of modern user experiences and the challenges we face developing user experiences that satisfy the needs of the end-user. It includes a demonstration of tools and techniques that can be used to reduce the risk of significant rework, resulting from changes in requirements for the UI of a system.

Chapter 4: Designing Software Systems That Age Well and Adapt to Change

Chapter 4 covers the nature of software rot and software entropy, its causes, and how we can approach decomposing a complex system to avoid this decay and enable sustainable business agility. A case study is used to provide context of these concepts and to do a deep dive into the principle of information hiding.

Chapter 5: Developers "Falling into the Pit of Success"

Chapter 5 discusses what happens when we do not put guard rails in place for our developers to ensure that the decisions they make will result in them "falling into the pit of success" as opposed to the "pit of failure." Several tools and techniques are demonstrated that will make it easier for a developer to do the right thing and not the wrong thing.

Chapter 6: Institutionalized Quality

Chapter 6 is dedicated to enforcing the concept that making quality a part of your culture requires that your processes and practices reflect a culture that values quality. This chapter reviews how this looks in an organization that has a culture that values quality.

Chapter 7: The Role of Chief Engineer

Chapter 7 demonstrates the importance of a chief engineer role who actively ensures the team is executing toward the outcomes everyone desires. This chapter outlines the key responsibilities for this role and the activities this person needs to perform.

Chapter 8: Bringing It All Together – Creating an Action Plan

Chapter 8 synthesizes the previous chapters into a series of considerations and approaches to develop an executable plan for transforming your organization based upon the most significant pain points. It ends with a discussion of what the developer experience will be like in this new organization.

—Doug Durham
Lincoln, Nebraska
April 5, 2021

CHAPTER 1

Focusing on Software Development Outcomes Instead of Outputs

Introduction

Imagine landscaping your yard is your hobby, and you would like to have a small storage building to keep all of your garden and yard tools organized and stored. You want to be the envy of your neighbors, so you take the opportunity to create something that will stand out. You spend an hour or two drawing something that demonstrates the style of the garden shed and its dimensions. Maybe something like the plans shown in Figure 1-1.

© Doug Durham and Chad Michel 2021
D. Durham and C. Michel, *Lean Software Systems Engineering for Developers*,
https://doi.org/10.1007/978-1-4842-6933-6_1

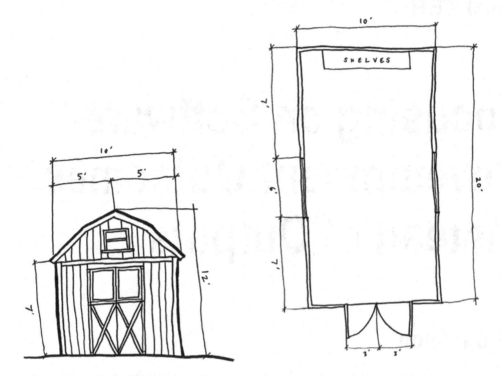

Figure 1-1. *Garden shed plans*

Let's say the design ends up being a 10' x 20' building. Given that you are more of a gardener than a carpenter, you reach out to some professionals to help you build this shed. You call your buddy, who is a carpenter, and he connects you with an electrician, plumber, concrete specialist, and painter who will help with the project. (I did say this needs to be the envy of your neighborhood, right?)

To kick off the project, you invite them over to collaborate on the drawings. You explain what you are looking for, and they ask the requisite questions about paint, windows, electrical outlet locations, etc., suggesting a few design improvements along the way. They estimate it will take them several days, maybe even a week, to finish the shed. Anxious to get started, you let them know that you are readily available to answer any questions and check in with them daily.

Fast-forward to the "reveal" of the finished garden shed. Ask yourself this: How likely do you think it will be that you will be happy with the garden shed, despite the fact there was very little planning and communication between you, as the designer/stakeholder, and the construction team? I suspect most, if not all of you would assume that the finished product would turn out great and your neighbors would, indeed, be duly impressed, just as you'd hoped. This is a very reasonable assumption. Even if the garden shed did turn out to disappoint, you can probably start over or make some changes without adding much cost or time.

Now, let's take it to the next level. Instead of building a garden shed, let's say you want to build an actual home. You go through the same process of spending a few hours making some drawings with dimensions and details you felt were important. You assembled your team of skilled craftsmen to review your drawings, and they ask more questions, then make more suggestions that improve (and even fix) some of your drawings and designs. They probably seem a little nervous about taking on a project like this given the size of the effort and the relatively small number of drawings (see Figure 1-2) and details being provided, but they finally agree to do it. They give you an estimate that you feel seems a little low given what you are envisioning, but you are not the expert, so you just assume that they know what they are doing.

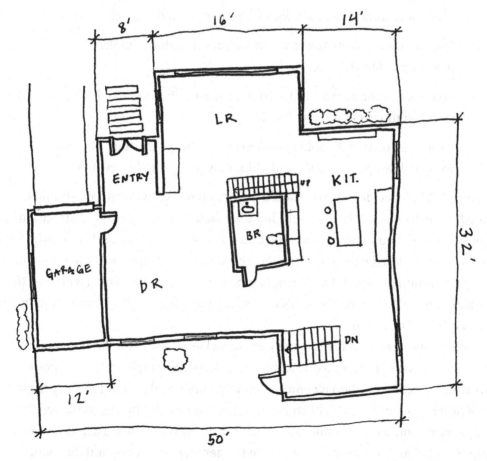

Figure 1-2. *Sketch for a house design*

As with the other scenario, you let them know that you are available for any questions that might come up and that you will be checking in with them on a weekly basis to see how things are going.

Fast-forward to the completion of the finished house. Consider this, how likely is it that you will be happy with the house? I suspect most, if not all of you, would have found the process of building the house frustrating and the finished product not what you envisioned. This is a very reasonable assumption.

Let's consider why that is and take a moment to hypothesize about where the project might have gone wrong:

- You might have assumed that the project would have started out fine as the foundation and other utilities work was done. After all, it does not really look like a house at this point and you are no expert, so what the contractors are doing is probably correct.

- Many decisions were made without your input and were clearly wrong.

- Some decisions were made without your input that actually improved the design of the house.

- Some of the contractors independently made choices that did not match your vision and resulted in a lot of rework.

- Other contractors did follow your vision without question, but they were bad design decisions and ultimately needed to be reworked.

In the end, you decide that you should have been more involved, you should have provided more details, you should have hired an architect and general contractor to ask the questions you didn't know to ask. Too much was left to chance and, as a result, your project took much longer, the costs greatly exceeded your budget, and you had to make so many compromises along the way that in the end you aren't satisfied with how the house looks and feels. You may even decide to sell the house and try again, thinking that you'll do it "right" next time.

Tackling complex projects the same way we tackle smaller, simpler projects will not work. As you can probably assume, while garden sheds might follow a process like what was described, when it comes to building houses, this is not the way these types of projects are executed. The most common scenario for house construction is to have a general contractor. It would be extremely uncommon to build a house without a complete set of architectural drawings that the general contractor and the team reference when constructing it (Figure 1-3).

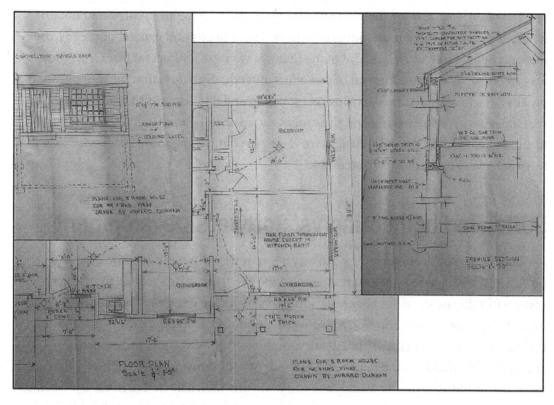

Figure 1-3. *Detailed house design*

The general contractor is also making sure that what is being built matches the plans and will be the person to go back to the owner with questions or suggestions. While the construction of the house is likely the largest overall expense, there is significant time and effort put into the planning portion that occurs prior to commencing construction. Clearly, building a house is a complicated endeavor, and leaving things to chance is a sure-fire way to run up the cost of the project and/or end up with a house that disappoints.

Modern software development is much the same way. When we think about the type of challenges we are faced with today and the types of problems we are trying to solve with software, is it building a garden shed or a home? Or, is the project complexity more akin to building a space station?

Using that analogy, let's think about how your projects are managed. Think about a project, small or complex, that you have worked on in the past. What was missing? Were your processes ill-defined or inconsistently followed? How much of the outcome of your projects was left to chance? Why was this? Did it make sense?

Too often, we are more focused on whether outputs are being created and not on whether the outcome of those outputs is meeting our needs and expectations. Yes, the house is being built and it has a lot of the features we were looking for. And true, there was an output of a house from all of this effort. But equally true is that the outcome of the process was unsatisfactory. Focusing on *outcomes* and not just *outputs* will help ensure that the efforts we are making and the processes we are following will align with our desired outcomes. In the end, the less we "leave to chance" the more successful we will be in achieving these desired outcomes.

Software Engineering vs. Software Development

Let's take a step back and examine the way we view the software development profession. We have all encountered people who call themselves software engineers instead of software developers or programmers. "Software engineer" sounds more formal and impressive compared to "software developer." You might think that getting the title of "software engineer" is a result of some formal education and/or some accredited evaluation of the depth and breadth of your skills. Sadly, the titles people are given in this industry are seemingly arbitrary and are often selected to make a job sound more impressive or to differentiate ourselves from others in the industry. Could you imagine this happening in other career fields? What if medical providers were allowed to pick their titles?

Imagine interviewing a variety of professionals across a broad spectrum of fields to understand what they do and what it means to be a doctor, or a lawyer, or a civil engineer. You might ask about their responsibilities, behaviors, and practices. It is safe to assume that you will get a consistent answer from all of the people you interview in each respective profession. Doctors are trained with similar methods and are exposed to a similar body of knowledge that they are trained on how to apply. Sure, they differ in the level of skill and their specialization and even in some of their techniques, but if you went to see a couple of orthopedic surgeons for an injury, you are likely to have a similar outcome regardless of whom you choose. These professions often include certification processes to ensure a minimum competency. The result is that there is a level of confidence and trust that the public has in these professions that (a) they are trained to a certain, consistent level, (b) they are competent practitioners of their profession, and (c) they leave little or nothing to chance. In fact, when someone from one of these professions fails to meet these expectations, it often makes the news or involves some legal processes. What if we, in the software development industry, were held to the same standards as doctors, lawyers, and engineers? Should we be held to similar standards? Wouldn't it be an improvement?

In order for our profession to mature and gain the respect and public confidence that other professions have, we must stop these informal practices. Titles must mean something. When we talk about what software engineering is, we should all be working from the same set of standards. We need to stop tolerating a lack of process and standardization in how we are building software. Anything short of this will simply perpetuate the pain we are currently feeling as a result of unpredictable and negative outcomes of our projects.

Coding Is Not Software Engineering

One of the contributing factors to this is that many, if not most, of our co-workers view coding as the principal activity of software engineering. If we don't have fingers on the keyboard, then we are not doing our job or creating value. We need to shake this notion.

Master Architect and IDesign founder Juval Löwy likes to say that coding is the "manufacturing" part of software development. This idea resonates with me and my background in the aircraft industry. Think about what it takes to build an airplane. Think about all of the people that are required to construct an airplane, from sheet metal workers, to welders and riveters, to people installing the hydraulics and electrical systems and all of the sensors, avionics, etc. Building an airplane is a complicated project, and airplanes themselves are complicated systems. While the people on the manufacturing floor (Figure 1-4) are clearly skilled and well trained (thank goodness!), I don't think anyone would give them the title of "aeronautical engineer." That title is reserved for those individuals who designed the airplane and created the plans and devised the processes that the technicians and assemblers use to build the plane.

Juice Flair/Shutterstock.com

Figure 1-4. *Airplane factory floor*

And yet, when we look at our own profession, we put a premium on the time we devote to writing code. Somehow, being productive in software development has been equated to the time our fingers are on the keyboard. Any other activities are looked upon as a hinderance to being productive. Output has been the focus. But, just as we would never start manufacturing an airplane without first performing the critical thought around planning for the design, development, and maintenance of the aircraft, we should be equally disciplined in how we approach software – that is, software engineering.

If you fail to plan, you are planning to fail.

—Benjamin Franklin

Defining Software Engineering

Rather than creating our own definitions of software engineering, we should embrace the definition put forth by the standards bodies that already exist. According to the Institute of Electrical and Electronics Engineers (IEEE), software engineering is

> *The application of a systematic, disciplined, quantifiable approach to the development, operation, and maintenance of software; that is, the application of engineering to software.*
>
> —ISO/IEC/IEEE Systems and Software Engineering Vocabulary and SWEBOK

When we break this down, a couple of things jump out right away. First, the scope of software engineering is inclusive of all phases of a software system: development, operation, and maintenance. This tells us that much more is involved in software engineering than just architecture or requirements analysis or coding. In fact, IEEE has identified 15 separate knowledge areas (KAs) in their latest version (V3.0) of the "Software Engineering Body of Knowledge," or SWEBOK[1] (Table 1-1). This should not surprise us if we are truly moving toward treating software as another engineering discipline. In this book, we are focused on about a third of these KAs and will touch on some of the others along the way.

Table 1-1. SWEBOK knowledge areas

Knowledge Area
Software Requirements
Software Design
Software Construction
Software Testing

(continued)

---

[1]P. Bourque and R.E. Fairley, eds., *Guide to the Software Engineering Body of Knowledge, Version 3.0*, IEEE Computer Society, 2014; www.swebok.org.

Table 1-1. *(continued)*

Knowledge Area
Software Maintenance
Software Configuration Management
Software Engineering Management
Software Engineering Process
Software Engineering Models and Methods
Software Quality
Software Engineering Professional Practice
Software Engineering Economics
Computing Foundations
Mathematical Foundations
Engineering Foundations

Note   The SWEBOK is an excellent source for authoritative references on topics in the KAs, and we strongly encourage you to familiarize yourself with this resource.

The second thing we might notice is the strong connection between software engineering and engineering in general through the phrase "the application of engineering to software." Software is not the unicorn that many would like us to believe. It does not have its own set of natural laws that it follows, separate from every other engineering discipline. The sooner we get away from this notion, the sooner we can start looking at other engineering disciplines (We're looking at you, systems engineering!) and adopt the best practices and lessons learned from these other disciplines, rather than re-learning them through trial and error.

So now that we have that out of the way, let's dig into the details of the attributes identified in the definition of a software engineering approach that is the "application of a systematic, disciplined, quantifiable approach to the development, operation, and maintenance of software." What does it mean for an approach to be systematic, disciplined, and quantifiable? To be systematic means to be methodical and to act according to a fixed plan or system. This means we need to have processes and practices (i.e., a "system") in place that allows us to take a methodical approach to the development, operation, and maintenance of software. This system should cover how we

- Define and analyze requirements

- Design our systems and architectures

- Design our software

- Construct our software

- Ensure our software is high quality

- Deploy our software

- Monitor our systems

- Manage our processes and projects

But we don't stop there: having a system is not enough. We have all seen organizations that have processes that no one follows. This is where "disciplined" comes into play. To be disciplined means we are showing a controlled form of behavior or way of working (reference definition source). To be disciplined means to do something consistently over time, both as individuals and as an organization. Everyone must be following the same system. This is how you get predictable outcomes – something we desperately need in our industry.

But how do we know what we are doing is working, and how can we continue to improve our systems and methods? This is where "quantifiable" comes into play. We need feedback loops for continuous improvement of our workers and processes, as well as to inform us on project progress and provide signals that help us detect when we are wandering off our plans and estimates. Inevitably, when we talk about metrics for software development, we start getting into massive debates about whether we are measuring the right things, how the measurements might be manipulated, concerns about using measurements to judge individual performance, and on, and on. We need to get past this and focus on those measurements that will help us understand how well our processes are working. Examples of these types of measurement metrics are

- Quality in the form of defect detection rates

- Budget against project plans

- Progress against project plans

- Productivity

- Effort spent on rework

- Accuracy of estimates

- Customer satisfaction

Why Does Software Engineering Matter?

In many ways, this is a great time to be in the software development industry. There is very little in our lives that has not been impacted by software. This change has been happening for a while. In 2011, Marc Andreessen wrote an essay titled "Why Software Is Eating the World."[2] It's a good read. His main point is that software has become pervasive throughout virtually every industry. It is necessary for innovation and provides competitive advantages. Software is impacting the business world like never before. What's more, we are now using software to solve problems that a few years ago seemed unimaginable; everything from self-driving cars to landing car-sized vehicles on Mars.[3] Small companies are developing novel technologies that are keeping us safer and making us more productive. Large companies are building platforms and infrastructure that enable us to avoid much of the burden of hosting and supporting our applications. Development tools and frameworks are reducing a lot of the "plumbing" that used to be required so that we can focus more on building features. It is tempting to feel like we are in a "golden age."

But there is a reality check we all need to take. Everything mentioned earlier is true, but it hides an ugly truth. While the complexity of the problems we are trying to solve has continually increased (and will continue), our ability to meet the challenge

---

[2]2011 August 20, *The Wall Street Journal*, Why Software Is Eating the World by Marc Andreessen, Quote Pages n/a, New York.

[3]www.jpl.nasa.gov/videos/curiositys-seven-minutes-of-terror

of this complexity is not sufficient. Hardly a day goes by where we are not seeing some high-profile software failure that has impacted our ability to check-in for a flight or connect to an essential service. Something as simple as tallying the votes from the Iowa caucuses in the 2020 presidential election made national news. Every one of these events leaves a stain on all of us in this industry and continues to erode the public trust in our profession.

The problem is that while the technology we are using has matured and grown, we have not. In many ways, we are still trying to build software using the ad hoc, brute-force, maverick programming techniques we have used since the 1980s. We are trying to build houses today the same way we were building garden sheds in the past. Complicating this is the fact that our computer science education programs at the college level have not addressed the problem. Most undergraduate degrees in computer science only require a single, three-credit-hour course on software engineering. It seems that our colleges and universities are more focused on training people to work on the manufacturing floor than in the design rooms with the other engineers.

Let's take a look at another analogy to help make this point. Football is a great example of a team sport that involves all players executing simultaneously. Kids are able to participate in this sport at a very young age through flag football programs at schools and organizations like the YMCA. They obviously are not hiring professional coaches for these teams. In almost all cases, one of the parents, who might be a football fan, will volunteer to "coach" their kids' team. You can probably imagine what practices are like. The coach probably develops a handful of plays and formations for offense and defense. Nothing too complicated, because remember, we are dealing with ten-year-olds. They try to get everyone to understand their position, but they keep it simple. Stand here. Get in the way of the defender. Run left. Run right. Often, the outcome of the game is pre-determined by whether one team has a kid (or maybe two) that is bigger and faster than the other kids, and every time that kid gets the ball, they make plays and score, regardless of what any of the other kids on the team do.

Now, let's contrast that to college football. It's the same sport, but there is very little in common with what you see on the youth football team and what you see at the elite college level. The rules are the same, but the game itself is orders-of-magnitude more complex as it becomes more challenging to succeed. Opposing teams analyze your strengths and weaknesses, identify your tendencies, and design plays and formations to exploit these to their advantage. We are no longer in a realm where a single talented individual can consistently carry the day, regardless of how the rest of the team performs. College football teams are great examples of activities that require a systematic, disciplined approach to be successful. If one person on a team fails to perform their role in a given play, it often means failure for the entire team. If someone does not understand what they are supposed to do in a play, it can impact their teammates' ability to perform. Football is highly orchestrated, even though the players must make snap judgments to adjust to their opponent's actions. Elite coaches obsess about all aspects of the student athlete and attempt to control what they eat, how much sleep they get, their schoolwork, and how they train and prepare. They understand what can happen if you leave too much to chance.

Each new opponent does not mean the coaches have to redesign their approach to playing the game. Coaching staffs will have a structure to their offense and defense that is unique to their style of coaching. They then adjust their structure to each opponent in the form of a game plan. They call this their offensive or defensive "system."

The most successful coaches at this elite level often talk about the importance of eliminating mistakes. It's the mistakes that are keeping them from victory and reaching their potential. These mistakes are the little errors in judgment that the players make when they are not sure what to do or are in a situation that has not been defined for them. The coaches talk about the amount of preparation that the players must do to study game films, practice plays, review game plans, etc. In other words, they want nothing left to chance.

Let's bring this back to software development. When we look at the way our industry, in general, is approaching the challenges and complexity we are facing, it's like we are trying to coach a professional football team, but we are treating it as if we are playing youth football. We are desperately looking to recruit that star programmer who can carry the day through their exceptional athleticism even though we are playing against professional opponents (i.e., the problems we are trying to solve). The approach we are taking may have worked 10 or 20 years ago, but the game has changed. We were playing youth football then, but now we are being asked to play a more complicated game. We need to develop a "system" and adjust our approach, but most software professionals are not doing that. The result is predictable. The less we follow a more systematic, disciplined approach (i.e., the more we leave to chance), the more errors in judgment (both seen and unseen) will occur within our teams and negatively impact the outcomes of our projects and products. This is a serious and existential crisis for some organizations. As their competitors mature their processes (and they will), they will expose and exploit weaknesses in the competition to create their own competitive advantage.

14

Errors in Judgment

Most problems with software are neither intentional nor malicious. Rather, it is a situation where an individual made an incorrect decision, either implicitly or explicitly, as a result of a lack of definition, a lack of experience, or a lack of knowledge. When we examine the problems that occur in the other professions, we see that errors in judgment are often the root cause. However, the delta comes with the relative infrequency of these occurring in the other professions compared to software development. Our expectation should not be the total elimination of errors in judgment (we are human after all) but in minimizing these errors in judgment to the point where they represent the exception rather than the rule.

It's just a fact that people have different levels of experience, and that experience impacts our judgment. As we gain more experience, we will naturally have fewer errors in judgment. The problem is we can't teach experience. It has to be experienced! What we can do is work to limit the impact of inexperience when our teammates are making decisions. To do this, we need to look at the other factors impacting judgment.

Lack of knowledge and lack of definition are things we can normalize across our organizations, so that should be where we focus. When we refer to lack of knowledge in this context, we mean the body of knowledge for software engineering. Improving our knowledge enables us to apply this knowledge to our software engineering approach.

When we refer to a lack of definition as part of the problem, we mean the gaps in the system that defines our approach or a lack of discipline in how we are applying that approach to our teams and projects. Whether we lack a defined system or are not following the system we have defined, the end result is errors in judgment and an increasing amount of our outcome that is left to chance. Our success in managing the complexity of the problems we are trying to solve will be unpredictable.

Where do these errors in judgment tend to manifest themselves? We would all be better off if these decisions were big and easy to spot, with a flashing red light that would highlight the decision and allow a more experienced person to detect the problem and make a correction. Unfortunately, these obvious types of errors in judgment are rare. Software decay and rot[4] occur over time via small decisions that seem innocuous and innocent. These design decisions could be related to how a system is decomposed, how a method signature is designed, how much data is passed around, how state is

---

[4]"Software decay and rot" refers to the slow deterioration in the quality of the code and design that occurs over time.

handled, etc. None of these decisions, by themselves, will create the negative outcomes we are experiencing. It is the summation of these decisions – death by a thousand cuts. And these judgment errors are occurring throughout the project. A 2017 study[5] looked to understand when and why "bad code smells" occur in software. One of their most surprising conclusions was that these code smells were first being introduced at the very beginning of the project, as opposed to being introduced in maintenance phases later on.

Note   A "code smell" is evidence of a poor design or coding decision that has made it into the system.

The decay becomes apparent over time. We start to realize that making changes is becoming more and more difficult as a result of the need to modify behavior and logic throughout the system in order to make this one small change. In other words, the code (and the system) has become more tightly coupled[6] and has lost cohesion.[7] A corollary to this would be changes that we make and test, only to find that the change created a bug in some other part of the system, and we were totally unaware that part would be impacted. As a result, our quality begins to suffer, and we end up spending a lot of our time doing rework.

Another way this decay becomes apparent is when it becomes very difficult for developers to reason (i.e., develop an understanding) about the system because it has become so complex that it is too difficult to understand by any one individual. Module or component structure is changed in such a way that we are not sure what modules are responsible for what behavior. Certain parts of the system become black boxes because very few people on the team "understand what's going on in there." There is no conceptual integrity[8] to the overall design of the system. As a result, our productivity begins to slow down.

Yet another indicator is that we find ourselves implementing features that were not consistent with the system's overall "design philosophy," if it ever had one. We do this because it has become cumbersome to follow the original design philosophy as the

---

[5]IEEE Transactions on Software Engineering, Vol. 43, No. 11, November 2017, When and Why Your Code Starts to Smell Bad (and Whether the Smells Go Away), pp. 1063–1088.

[6]The level of coupling refers to the strength of the relationship between two pieces of code.

[7]The degree of cohesion refers to how closely related the code is within a module, class, etc.

[8]A design with conceptual integrity is one that is consistent and gives the impression there was a single designer.

software has matured, so we take some "shortcuts." We often say that in systems like this, it becomes easier for the developer to do the wrong thing instead of the right thing.

Most of us can easily identify projects in our experience that share these same manifestations. Here is an example I think will illustrate this in a way that will resonate with most people.

A few years ago, I was part of a team that was building an ecommerce platform that would be used by other software developers to sell their software online. It was a re-write of the original version of this system, made using Microsoft's Active Server Pages. We needed to move it to Microsoft's new (at the time) .NET framework in order to extend the system and add more sophisticated capabilities. The first design (Figure 1-5) of this system was very clean and understandable. We were quite proud of our design and thought it would be a strong, solid platform for growth.

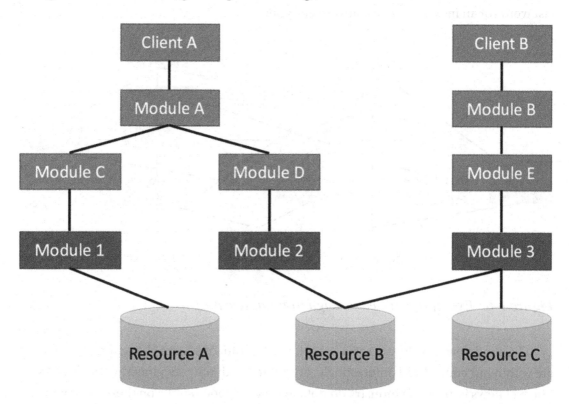

Figure 1-5. *Example of a clean and understandable design*

As expected, we continued to enhance and extend this system to add more features and capabilities. At the time, each of these new features was added with some modifications to the existing code, as well as the addition of some additional code and classes. Along the way, we felt like we were making solid trade-offs when we found our existing system needed to be modified to accommodate the new changes. Sure, sometimes we took some shortcuts and sometimes we did something that we knew was outside the normal pattern of the overall design, but we felt it was going to be too much work to "follow the patterns" in those cases. One small exception is not going to make much of a difference, right? What could go wrong?

I think you probably know how this story ended up. Within a few years, a "clean" and understandable design had transformed into a Frankenstein monster (Figure 1-6). We woke up one day and realized we had a mess on our hands. Generally, this epiphany occurs when someone asks for a feature that would require so much rework and so much redesign that we look at it and realize that it might be almost as much work to simply rewrite the whole system. But of course, this time we would do it right! Famous last words of an inexperienced software designer.

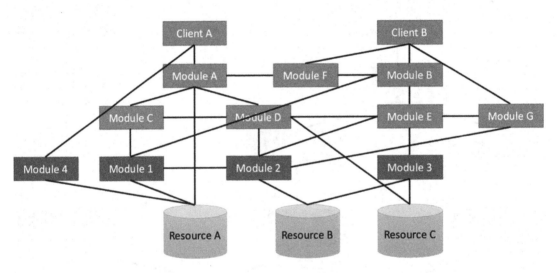

Figure 1-6. *Example of a clean design that has decayed*

The good news is software rot is a result of a handful of system characteristics that are within our control and, interestingly, are shared with other engineering disciplines. The bad news is, we as an industry do not have a very good handle on these concepts. The concepts of coupling, cohesion, and conceptual integrity (along with information hiding) are so important to fully and deeply understand that we are devoting an entire chapter to them in this book.

Managing the Dimensions of Complexity in Software Development

Given all the variables involved in software development, from people to problem domains, to technologies and processes, it should come as no surprise that the complexity that must be managed in software development is diverse. In order to target complexity as something that should be actively managed, it is helpful to organize our understanding of complexity into a finite number of dimensions.

Objective Complexity

Objective complexity encapsulates organizational structural realities or domain-specific complexities that may not be directly related to specific functional requirements. It is often focused on answering the "why" of initiatives and gives context for the "what."

A shared understanding of this type of complexity creates deeper empathy and helps us make better, more well-informed decisions. Examples of this type of complexity are shown in Table 1-2.

Table 1-2. *Examples of objective complexity*

Source	Rationale
The vision, mission, and values of an organization	These must be understood so that any solution is authentic, aligned, and advances the agenda of the organization.
The stage of the business and its decision-making and organizational structure	This will influence communication patterns, stakeholder involvement, project stage-gates, etc.
Selection and prioritization of initiatives	Organizations always have more opportunities than resources available. The reasoning behind the selection of an initiative must be understood to ensure the sustainability of the initiative. There is generally an impact/outcome that is desirable, and the challenge becomes creating the right outputs to fulfill them.

(continued)

Table 1-2. (*continued*)

Source	Rationale
Community, sustainability, and social impacts	These are frequently considered in communication, product development, and product function.
Regulatory, legal, or other strategic considerations	For example, the old Microsoft would have refused to embrace Linux as part of their solution mix. We may favor one vendor over another due to a relationship and not cost/function considerations.
Marketing and branding standards	These may narrow the range of acceptable solutions within an initiative or directly influence specific functionality (it must be fun, it must be serious, etc.).
Metrics of success	Understanding the impact that is desired and the metrics that will be used to measure the success and impact of the software project on the business.
Build vs. buy	Understanding the relative importance of proprietary features and capabilities that can push a decision toward build vs. buy. Do these proprietary features represent competitive advantages and intellectual property, or are they more in the realm of preferences? Understanding the desired business outcome is critical.

Requirements Complexity

Requirements complexity represents the challenges with understanding *what* we should be building. We are all familiar with the situations where stakeholders struggle to provide the necessary details for what is needed or can't agree on the requirements. Requirements complexity comes in many forms beyond these two more common challenges. Some examples are shown in Table 1-3.

Table 1-3. *Examples of requirements complexity*

Source	Rationale
Stakeholder alignment	Ensuring that the goals of the stakeholders who are depending on the software are fully understood by everyone involved. This could also lead to an inability to commit to a specific set of requirements.
Multidisciplined stakeholders	Challenges around the fact that many projects have multiple stakeholders, and these stakeholders can be coming from a variety of different roles within an organization. This could mean they can have conflicting goals and objectives.
Emerging requirements	Given that many software projects represent solutions to complex problems, it should be expected that new, unforeseeable requirements might reveal themselves during the development phase of a project.
Blind spots	Requirements that are there at the beginning but tend to hide in the "nooks and crannies" and are very difficult to see and tease out, but then present themselves during development and end up forcing a significant amount of rework because they are absolutely required.
Product market/ customer fit	Difficulties with validating that what has been designed will meet the needs of the target customers. Use of low-fidelity prototypes is helpful, but many users will not be able to provide the feedback you need until they see some working software.
Increased need for UI/UX sophistication	Understanding the relative importance of proprietary features and capabilities that can push a decision toward build vs. buy. Do these proprietary features represent competitive advantages and intellectual property, or are they more in the realm of preferences? Understanding the desired business outcome is critical.

Solution Complexity

Solution complexity represents the challenges with *how* we should build what we are building. Like requirements complexity, solution complexity comes in many forms and presents a number of challenges. Some examples are shown in Table 1-4.

Table 1-4. Examples of solution complexity

Source	Rationale
Quality	Designing systems and creating development environments that enable testing throughout development.
Hosting platforms & technologies	The explosion of hosting options and platform-as-a-service (PAAS) capabilities of modern cloud platforms can be overwhelming.
Performance and scale	The need to design and host systems in such a way that when performance and scale requirements need to be addressed, there are options that allow these to be addressed without requiring changes to the software.
Security	Ensuring the sensitive data and functionality that our systems contain are protected from exploitation or unauthorized access.
Maintainability/ Readability	Designing applications that are easy to reason about and that enable extensibility and modification over the lifetime of the application without degradation of velocity of the development team.
Design integrity	Having, and maintaining, a software architecture and software design that follows a single set of design ideas and looks as if it was designed and built by a single individual.
UI sophistication	Managing the growing demands being placed on UI developers.
Complex algorithms or workflows	Effectively managing the essential complexity of the key value propositions and features of the system.
Targeting multiple platforms	The need to create applications that support multiple clients (e.g., browser, mobile, tablet).

Agility Comes from Managing Both Requirements and Solution Complexity

When it comes to managing complexity within software development itself, we think of this complexity as falling into two of these three dimensions: requirements complexity and solution complexity. The industry has spent a lot more effort over the last 20 years focusing on the adoption of processes and methods to help manage requirements complexity. The explosion of methodologies, tools, education, and coaching consultants that have followed the agile movement is evidence of this focus.

Unfortunately, the story is not the same for managing solution complexity. While there has been tremendous growth in cloud technologies, CI/CD platforms, programming languages, development environments, and frameworks, the development of accompanying methods and processes and the adoption of best practices to enable our industry to effectively design and build applications using this technology has, by and large, been neglected. Part of this neglect could be a result of the emphasis on frameworks over the last 10–15 years. It seems like there is always something new coming out that promises to make it easier to develop this type of application or that type of application. Anyone who has used one of these frameworks will realize it's just as easy to develop a giant ball of mud within a framework as it is without one. It's like a painter claiming, "I would be a better artist if I had a better paintbrush!"

Note   Frameworks are a tool, not a solution. No framework is going to solve our solution complexity problems until we learn how to effectively use them from a software engineering standpoint. In other words, we need to first have the systematic and disciplined software engineering approach in place, and then we can leverage the frameworks as a tool for managing complexity.

A few years ago, I was invited to attend a "launch party" for a local organization that was just completing the implementation of its new agile methodology. There was a lot of excitement within the team. You could tell they were very optimistic about how these new processes and methods would give them a competitive advantage in their market. They were looking forward to increased release frequency and being able to rapidly turn around new features for their customers. I was excited for them as well. I sought out one of their technical leaders to find out more about what they were doing. Knowing that they did not have a strong software engineering culture, I wanted to find out what they had done to help ensure the "continuous attention to technical excellence and good design" that the authors of the Agile Manifesto[9] listed as a key principle behind agility. Sadly, they had not given any thought to changing anything in terms of how they were going to design, build, and test the software that was going to emerge from their new agile world. I left that event feeling bad for them, knowing that they would be facing some tough realities.

---

[9]www.agilemanifesto.org

It has to be the goal of every development team, whether stated or not, to be as productive and responsive in version 100 of an application as in version 1. No one wants to be a part of a team that is constantly bogged down and having to make excuses for why it will take so long to add this feature or that feature. In the end, four fundamental challenges keep teams from being able to maintain a constant velocity in perpetuity, the inability to

- Manage the level and type of coupling in a system

- Enable a system to change over time while preserving conceptual integrity

- Effectively manage system and application state

- Proficiently achieve desired system quality

Agility comes from effectively managing both *requirements complexity* AND *solution complexity*. Implementing an agile process without first transforming the development team will not end well. A development team needs to be able to design, build, and maintain software that can be extended and enhanced indefinitely.

Our Responsibility

If we want to be well regarded as a profession, we need to start embracing a notion of responsibility. This means taking ownership of our roles as software developers in the organizations and enterprises where we work and are continually working to gain the trust of our customers.

What, specifically, are these responsibilities? If we look at this from the outside in, what most customers want from us is *predictable outcomes*, the *ability to respond quickly and effectively* to opportunities (something we call sustainable business agility), and improved *visibility to enable informed decision-making*.

Predictable outcomes refer to the ability to agree with stakeholders on the value we intend to create (i.e., the outcome) and then execute on time, on budget, and delivering the envisioned value. It's what happens when you contract with a builder, and they deliver the house you wanted on time and on budget. It's being reliable so that the rest of the business can trust us and make plans based upon that trust.

Sustainable business agility refers to our ability to consistently respond to changes as a result of new opportunities for the business (i.e., new features or enhancements). When the business sees an opportunity, they are going to want to quickly and efficiently capitalize on that opportunity. If our response is that it will take longer than expected because our system has become difficult to change or that our development resources are having to spend a lot of their time supporting the production system, then we are falling short of meeting our responsibility.

Just because we have taken the steps necessary to effectively manage the complexity of our projects, it does not mean they will be without challenges. We will still be faced with requirements that reveal themselves during development, changes as a result of user testing, estimates that were outside our normal range of accuracy, developers who are not able to devote the time we expected to the project, and so on. When situations like these have the potential to materially impact our project plans, it is necessary for us to address them with the broader audience, including stakeholders outside the development team. One of the first things they will want to know is the scope of the impact in some quantifiable, non-technical way. This is where our responsibility for providing improved visibility can help with decision-making. Whether it's *burndown charts*[10] or *earned value charts*[11] or some other reporting mechanism, we need to demonstrate progress and remaining work in an accurate format so that all the project stakeholders have the confidence to use this data to understand the impact of change and make decisions.

Effectively managing complexity, meeting our responsibilities, and gaining the respect of our customers and the public requires changes to our current approach. We need to reduce errors in judgment and take control of our development efforts in a way that minimizes what is left to chance and creates predictable outcomes for our stakeholders.

A Path Forward

Much like a football coach, we need to start by focusing on the outcomes we desire and then creating the systematic, disciplined approaches that will lead us to these outcomes. Along the way, we need to make sure we are measuring those things that help us fine-tune our approach and tell us how well we are doing. In the next five chapters, we will dive into five key outcomes (Figure 1-7) that dramatically improve your ability to create both predictable project outcomes as well as sustainable business agility, even as the complexity of the problems we are solving continues to increase.

---

[10]www.agilealliance.org/glossary/burndown-chart/

[11]www.pmi.org/learning/library/earned-value-management-systems-analysis-8026

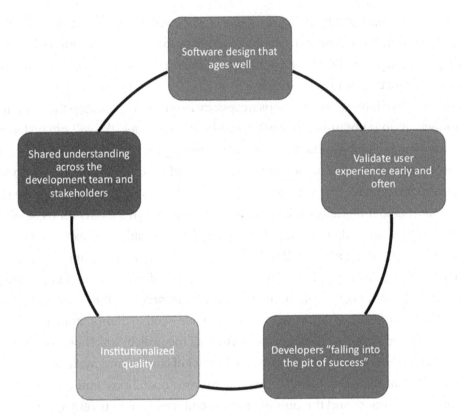

Figure 1-7. *Five outcomes that improve the odds of predictable project outcomes and sustainable business agility*

One thing to keep in mind with these outcomes is that they do not reflect discrete phases during development, but rather they span the entire development timeline and lifecycle. This is important to understand because it reinforces that software development is a team-based activity that is highly dependent upon effective communication and processes. The end result is a highly integrated, dependent relationship between the processes, outputs, and outcomes that we, collectively as a team, are pursuing. Anyone looking for a single silver bullet to solve problems will not find it here. The problems we face are multi-dimensional, and the solution is thus multi-dimensional. It takes devotion, discipline, surveillance, coaching, teaching, and nurturing.

What we will end up with is a hybrid approach to designing and building software that combines modern lean processes with disciplined software engineering and design. This unique combination enables several consistent and critical outcomes:

- The most valuable capabilities and features of the system are delivered to end-users quickly and with a high degree of quality.

- End-user feedback is rapidly incorporated into the backlog prioritization process.

- The design of the system responds to new priorities and capabilities without compromising the conceptual integrity of the design or requiring "re-architecting" the system later.

By integrating these two disciplines of software development, you can effectively minimize decisions and outcomes left to chance to create an environment where effective management of both requirements and solution complexity is the norm.

Summary

Software engineering is more than just a fancy title to make ourselves sound important or professional. It needs to mean something to call ourselves software engineers. If the definition of software engineering is "the application of a systematic, disciplined, quantifiable approach to the development, operation, and maintenance of software," then calling yourself a software engineer means you are devoted to the practice and dedicated to the principles behind it.

More than ever, we need software engineering to build modern, complex software that is easily maintained and enhanced time and again, and a big part of that is providing predictable outcomes and business agility for our efforts.

Key Takeaways

- **Being a software engineer means we are leaving nothing to chance** and are working to minimize errors in judgment. It exemplifies being systematic and disciplined.

- **Complexity comes in multiple forms,** and our success is dependent on our ability to effectively manage complexity related to requirements and solutions.

- **Predictable results occur when we take control of our development processes** and minimize or eliminate weaknesses in the process that lack structure and discipline.

- **Focusing our efforts on achieving desired outcomes can identify gaps** in our processes and show the value of the activities and outputs we are creating.

- **Integrating lean processes and disciplined software engineering and design is necessary** to effectively manage the complex problems we are trying to solve in modern applications.

- **Processes and practices do not exist in a vacuum.** There is an integrated, co-dependent relationship between what we are doing and the ultimate predictability and agility we seek. Understanding this helps us achieve the discipline needed within individuals and the team.

With a foundation of understanding the importance of focusing on outcomes and the need for a disciplined process to achieve predictable results, we'll now turn our attention to our first desired outcome, gaining a shared understanding.

CHAPTER 2

Gaining a Shared Understanding Throughout the Project

Introduction

Any intelligent fool can make things bigger and more complex... It takes a touch of genius – and a lot of courage to move in the opposite direction.

—E.F. Schumacher

Writing is nature's way of letting you know how sloppy your thinking is.

—Dick Guindon

As my oldest child became a teenager, he wanted to learn how to drive a car with a manual transmission. We have a Jeep Wrangler with a six-speed that is not necessarily the easiest thing to learn on but was an adequate "lab" for learning this skill. We went to a large parking lot near our house. I drove the car around a bit and explained the interaction between the stick shift, my left foot on the clutch, and my right foot on the accelerator. My son is mechanically inclined, so he soaked this all up and we decided to change places and see how he did. As expected, the first few attempts resulted in the car lurching forward and stalling because he took his foot off the clutch too fast. No problem! We discussed how the clutch and accelerator had to interact to create the smooth transition from stopped to moving in first gear. He nodded, indicating he understood. Things were going great!

© Doug Durham and Chad Michel 2021
D. Durham and C. Michel, *Lean Software Systems Engineering for Developers*,
https://doi.org/10.1007/978-1-4842-6933-6_2

This cycle of stop, lurch, stall continued for some time. He would be successful getting it going for a time, but then there would be a series of lurches and stalls. I explained again how the release of the clutch needed to coincide with a depression of the accelerator. He seemed to understand but could not put this into practice. Morale was declining. We gave up for the day.

My son went home and watched videos that described how a manual transmission worked, thinking that he just needed to better understand the mechanical interaction of the system. I applauded him for that but assured him that you did not have to be a mechanical engineer (what he is today!) to drive a stick shift. We went out again, a few days later, but we had a similar outcome. This was just a skill that was going to take some practice to get right.

On our third outing, starting with the same problems, he asked if I could drive so that he could watch my feet. I thought this was odd, but worth a shot. Once he saw how my feet interacted with the pedals and could hear the corresponding engine sounds, the light bulb turned on for him. The next time he got into the driver's seat, he was on his way and has never looked back. It was a remarkable experience to see him suddenly "get it." All of my very "clear," "accurate," and "descriptive" verbal directions of how to drive were not enough for him to develop an accurate mental model for how the process worked. It took something else, something more visual, to connect what I was saying with what he needed to do. Despite the assumption that we had a shared understanding, he clearly had a flawed mental model that was not going to change, no matter how many different ways I tried to explain it. He needed to see something that challenged what he "thought" I was telling him to do, to allow us to understand where our mental models differed. This technique of watching my feet was a successful approach for teaching our other children, as well.

In the previous chapter, we discussed the fact that the types of problems we are trying to solve today continue to become more complex. Steve McConnell, in his book *Code Complete*,[1] referred to the nature of software design as a wicked problem – a problem where the solution is not found until the problem is solved. As complexity increases, the important details and information necessary to solve the problem also increase (just as we pointed out in building a garden shed vs. a house). In this chapter, we will discuss why it is important for us to develop a shared understanding around this complexity. We then dive into specific techniques that will increase the shared understanding to achieve the predictable outcomes we are seeking.

---

[1]McConnell, Steven C. 2004. *Code Complete*, 2nd ed. Microsoft Press.

Sources of Defects and Rework

We have not completed an actual scientific survey but are confident that if you asked the average person, "What is the main source of defects in software?" they would likely say, "sloppy coding" or "logic errors." They would be wrong! Research varies on this topic, but empirical studies have shown that coding errors are the source of only a portion of bugs. Requirements and design are implicated in a large percentage of bugs, with some studies showing them responsible for more than 50% of all defects. What's more, these types of defects tend to be the most severe, the hardest to prevent, and the most expensive to correct.

This is an interesting statistic that should give us pause. Why are we having so many defects related to requirements, if adopting agile methods are supposed to help us manage requirements complexity? But let's take a look at another metric – rework.

Rework is defined as required changes to the software that occur after a developer asserted the work was complete and correct. In other words, the developer has submitted their code changes and indicated that they are done with that work and ready to move on to the next task. Many organizations find themselves spending 50% or more of their development effort on rework. Those numbers are frightening. On average, more than half of our development resources are fixing problems with existing code instead of developing new features. This should be unacceptable. At our worst, we should be targeting percentages around 20%-25%.

The good news is that reducing rework represents an enormous opportunity to increase our productivity without increasing headcount or forcing people to work more hours. For example, if a four-person team can reduce their rework from 50% to 25%, they have effectively added another developer and increased their capacity for feature development by 50%. Figure 2-1 illustrates this impact. It's significant. Reducing rework will be a recurring theme throughout this book. If you are not tracking this metric, you should begin. We discuss the tracking of key metrics in Chapter 8.

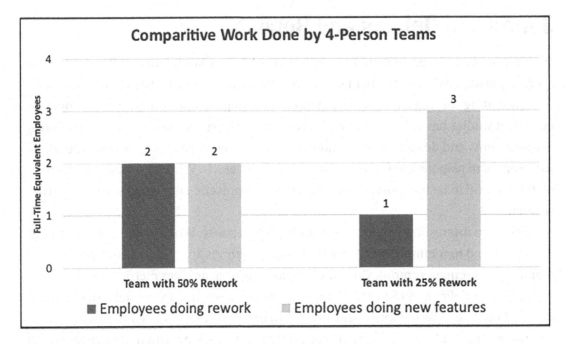

Figure 2-1.   *Impact of rework on a four-person team*

We have established that it is desirable to reduce rework and requirements are a significant source of defects (a.k.a. rework), but what is the real problem, and how can we improve this? Isn't this more of a product management or product owner problem? The short answer is that the development team must drive the changes that need to be made, not the product owner. But before we get into that, let's talk about why the problem exists.

The Danger of Incomplete Pictures

One of the benefits of embracing agile methods is that we have brought stakeholders and developers closer together and allowed them to communicate more freely. We have all probably seen the brainstorming sessions of product folks and tech folks huddled around a wall with a flurry of post-it notes laying out a brief description of some feature or user story. There are lots of conversations taking place around what the one-line description of a story or feature represents. Let's use a fictional scenario to observe how these conversations might progress. I will be using graphics instead of words to represent an abstraction of the feature definition.

The product owner, who has spent a fair amount of time thinking about and researching this new feature, has developed their mental model of what the feature looks like. Figure 2-2 represents what the product owner "sees" in their mind's eye.

Figure 2-2. *Product owner's mental model of the feature*

When you and the product owner have a conversation about this feature, they go into great detail to describe the feature and walk you through how it should work and the benefit that the customer will get from having this feature in the software. Along the way, you ask some clarifying questions. At the end, you feel like you have a good handle on this feature and the product owner feels like you are both "on the same page" and have a shared understanding. Figure 2-3 represents your mental model of the feature, overlaid with the mental model of the product owner. As you can see, there is quite a bit of overlap between your two models. However, there are some assumptions you have implicitly made that cause your model to expand beyond the borders of the product owner's model. Additionally, there are some details that the product owner failed to mention, which results in some parts of your model not overlapping with theirs.

Figure 2-3. *Product owner's mental model vs. your mental model*

During development, you are working with the quality assurance (QA) person responsible for testing the new feature. Another conversation occurs where you describe the feature, answer some of their questions, and agree that you both have a good handle on the feature and how it behaves so that they can run some acceptance tests. Figure 2-4 shows all three of these mental models. As expected, there is a continued divergence of understandings.

Figure 2-4. *Adding the QA engineer's mental model*

It would be fair to equate what we have described with the game "telephone," where people sit around a table and one person starts by whispering something quickly into their neighbor's ear, and this continues around the circle until you get to the last person, and they must say what they heard. Often, the original message is quite different from what the last person thought they heard. The difference in our example is that the message isn't really being distorted. We are using verbal conversation to try and create a shared understanding. In fact, the aggregate of the three mental models likely represents a more complete picture of the true requirements (see Figure 2-5). If only these three people could express their mental models in a way that we could create this aggregation.

Figure 2-5. *The aggregate of all three mental models*

Given the problems we have had in creating a shared understanding, we can only assume the complete picture of the real feature requirements probably looks something like Figure 2-6. In Chapter 5 we will discuss tools and techniques we can use during the development phase to help reveal more of the complete picture.

Figure 2-6. *The "complete picture"*

As you read this scenario, you were probably nodding in agreement because you have experienced something like this happening. Most of us have also had a conversation like the following:

Product Owner: "Hey, I just looked at the Edit Order feature on QA and noticed it didn't allow me to adjust the quantity of an item on an order. Are you still working on that?"

You: "No, I'm done with the Edit Order feature. When we talked through what this needed to do, you never mentioned the need to adjust the quantity. When did this change?"

Product Owner: "Nothing has changed. I just assumed it was obvious that if you could delete an item on an order, you should also be able to adjust the quantity. Is this going to be a big deal to add?"

You: "Well, yes, I have already moved on to something else in this next sprint. How important is this?"

Product Owner: "Very. We can't release this until it's fixed."

The bottom line is that while verbal communication is the easiest way for us to interact with others, it is insufficient for the exchange of detailed information and creating a shared understanding. As humans, we have biases that impact our perceptions (such as Attentional and Anchoring[2]) that can make it difficult for us to see all of the details and variations when we are trying to understand what someone is describing. When we rely solely on verbal communication, we are terrible about identifying and expressing details in a structured way that would ensure a comprehensive and complete description. People do not intend to be vague or misleading. They are honestly trying to cover all of the details. No one has anything to gain by holding information back. However, this failure to recognize the biases and bad assumptions leads to the vast majority of rework related to requirements. You can boil this down into two pitfalls which we call "The Danger of Incomplete Pictures":

> Our assumption that we all have a shared picture.

> Our assumption that all assumptions and requirements are known.

Why Developing a Shared Understanding Early Is Important

There are people who will tell you that spending a lot of time trying to understand requirements before coding is wasteful and should be avoided. They argue that we should embrace the idea that requirements will "emerge" as we begin producing working software and the users start providing feedback. We will be blunt: this is a naïve and dangerous position to take.

Too many software systems being developed today are done in such a way that very little time is devoted upfront to requirements analysis or design. Instead, someone starts to build something in order to get user feedback on what the other requirements should be. It's almost like they have struggled with the idea of critical thought and planning, so they have just thrown up their hands and made some excuse about this being the nature of software. "It's a wicked problem, dude!" Could you imagine if this is how they decided to build the software for the auto-landing system of the Mars Curiosity rover? Or the flight control system of a commercial aircraft? Or maybe the heart rate monitor used in hospitals? Or the house we discussed in Chapter 1? No engineer would do it this way. And if someone makes the argument that software is different than those types of systems because software is "easy to change," the person who is trying to make a simple

---

[2]www.psychologytoday.com/us/basics/bias

change in that giant ball of mud created four years ago would beg to differ. If you want a good argument, then read Turing Award winner Leslie Lamport's essay "Why we should build software like we build houses."[3]

The whole argument behind this notion that we should just start coding seems to be built upon the idea that requirements inevitably change, so why spend time trying to identify all requirements? It thus implies that most requirements are not knowable prior to development. We know from experience that this is patently false. It is true that some requirements are created or revealed during development as we use the working software and see opportunities that we had not considered. These tend to be a very small percentage of what we could consider the total requirements for the system being built.

A more accurate way to view the requirements conundrum and the fact that we have so much rework associated with requirements is to say that, using our current processes, many requirements are not *revealed* until we are in development. A requirement that is revealed is a requirement that can be known during our planning stages. A technique called the Johari Window[4] can be a useful visualization of where these requirements are that get revealed during development (Figure 2-7).

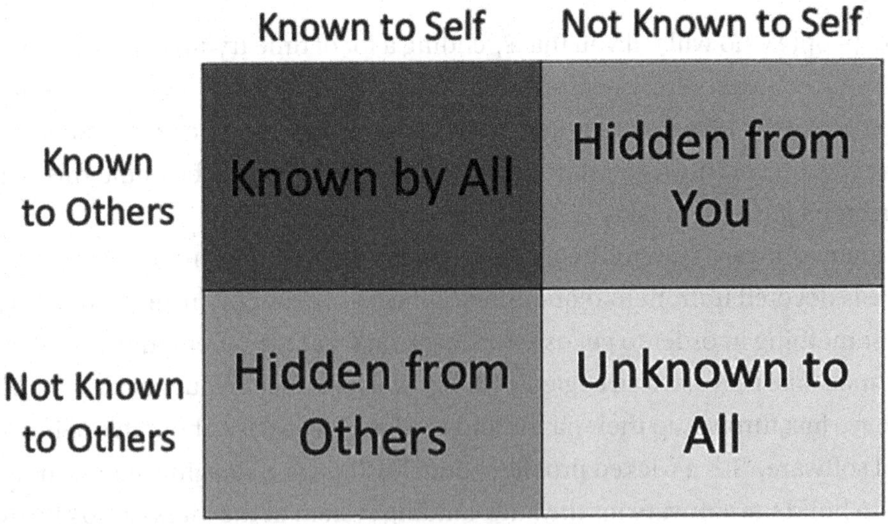

	Known to Self	Not Known to Self
Known to Others	Known by All	Hidden from You
Not Known to Others	Hidden from Others	Unknown to All

Figure 2-7. *Using the Johari window to visualize the nature of shared understanding of requirements*

[3]www.wired.com/2013/01/code-bugs-programming-why-we-need-specs/
[4]https://en.wikipedia.org/wiki/Johari_window

The overlap between our mental models represents "Known by All," those pieces of information that are both known to ourselves as well as to others. In any conversation, we will be successful in sharing information so that there is a shared understanding of these "Knowns."

On the other end of the spectrum are those requirements that are not known to you or others. These are the "Unknown to All" (also known as "Unknown Unknowns" made famous by Donald Rumsfeld when he was Secretary of Defense in 2002[5]). The folks arguing for skipping planning and requirements analysis are treating most requirements as falling into this category. It is true, we should not focus our attention on identifying requirements that are not knowable, but as we discussed earlier, not all requirements are unknowable.

The illustration in Figure 2-7 represented a scenario where three people all had mental models of a feature that differed. These differences are represented in the Johari window by the remaining two squares.

The first are those requirements that are known to you but not known to others. We label those "Hidden from Others" because they represent information that we have, but are not effectively sharing with others. Again, this is not intentional. It's just the nature of how we view complexity and the inefficiency in how we express complex concepts verbally.

The second and final square represents those requirements that are known to others but not known to you. These are labeled "Hidden from You" because we cannot see them even though they are there.

Clearly, these two areas are where we should focus our attention. These requirements are known to someone, so we need to apply tools and techniques that will allow them to surface and be understood and shared by all. Every one of these requirements that is revealed prior to the coding phase represents a reduction in the unnecessary development volatility and rework.

Adding Structured Processes

Relying primarily on mental models as described in the preceding scenario means being okay with ambiguity and the high likelihood that you and your stakeholders will not achieve much of a shared understanding prior to development. Alternatively, if we are to use some tools and techniques that require us to articulate our thoughts in a structured

---

[5]www.scientificamerican.com/article/rumsfelds-wisdom/

way (i.e., write them down), we will begin to see how much more detail is revealed and ultimately shared. Our abstract mental model transitions to a more concrete and shared understanding that can be inspected and critiqued by others. No doubt you have experienced this when you jumped into coding something that you thought you understood but discovered additional details and considerations along the way. Writing code is a structured process that forces us to consider things in more detail (e.g., branching in logic you had not considered).

This use of structured techniques often reveals gaps in our understanding of the problem or solution – important gaps that are valuable to identify early on. In the remainder of this chapter, we will present two separate activities that should occur early in a project. These activities can significantly improve shared understanding of requirements compared to relying primarily on verbal interactions. The key is to use tools and techniques that force our minds to dig into the details and express them in a way that fosters critical thinking by ourselves and the rest of the team. As a bonus, these techniques can also bring forward conversations and analysis that can lead to uncovering those requirements that fall in the "Unknown to All" square and increase the shared understanding of the business domain by all team members.

Leveraging Lean Approaches to Backlog Development

Most modern development teams are working from a backlog of stories and epics that (in most cases) are developed by product owners or some other stakeholder or subject matter expert (SME). These individuals often have some training in story development, enabling them to write a correctly formatted user story and, hopefully, including some acceptance criteria.

These stories then get prioritized and committed to sprints. Developers pick them off the storyboard and develop them. Code gets pushed to QA, and the developer demos the features in a sprint review. This process will sound familiar to anyone in an agile environment.

As we established earlier, these types of discrete interactions and handoffs are prone to problems related to a lack of a shared mental model between stakeholders and the development team. The larger the team involved, the bigger the problems become. The problems on the developer side are generally related to a lack of a shared understanding of the context for the feature they are implementing.

Context is an extremely important concept when building something as part of a team. Imagine you are tasked with building a liquid cooling system for some unknown device in order to keep the temperature between 50 and 75 degrees. Given that the temperature range is pretty narrow, you decide to create a water-based cooling system because that would be the least expensive and simplest approach (i.e., being agile!). You assume (maybe implicitly) that this device is being used indoors somewhere since that has been your experience with previous projects. You deliver this to the customer only to find out the device to be cooled is located outdoors and in a location with hot summers and frigid winters. A little understanding of the overall use case would have been nice, right? Sure, you could have asked the questions yourself, but that only seems obvious in retrospect.

Let's look at a software example. Say you are asked to create an application that allows you to assist with performing maintenance on mechanical devices by enabling the ability to look up the device details and record details of the maintenance as it is being performed. Pretty straightforward. We will need a server (likely in the cloud) that will host an API that our web client will access for device lookups and to post events related to the maintenance of the device. You are quite proud of yourself for realizing that the user will probably be using a tablet or mobile phone to do these queries, so you make sure the web application is responsive (even though no one asked for this). Only later, after the system has been deployed for testing, do you find out that some of these devices are located in remote areas that have no Internet connection or cell coverage. The stakeholder might have even known this but did not think it was relevant information, or it did not occur to them to mention these scenarios since they were only focused on a small set of core use cases.

Both of these are concrete examples of the danger of incomplete pictures and hidden assumptions discussed before. There was a fair amount of overlap in the shared understanding that was "Known by All," but some critical requirements were "Hidden from You" that were clearly knowable before development began.

Solving these types of problems (i.e., increasing the overlap of mental models) requires that development teams and stakeholders take active, structured steps to surface the questions that will lead to the identification of these requirements that are "Hidden from Others" or "Hidden from You." The primary goal of this first set of activities, journey and story mapping, is to (1) create a complete set of high-level stories and epics and (2) create the shared understanding of the context in which these stories and epics exist. The second set of activities, decomposing and estimating stories, helps reveal hidden assumptions and details that are not consistently revealed at the story/epic level.

Journey Mapping and Story Mapping

One of the best techniques we have found to start this process is to employ a technique called journey mapping.[6] In this process, members of the development team, along with UI/UX designers, product owners, and stakeholders, get together to co-create a visual representation of the journey that an end-user takes through the process that includes the software to be developed. Figure 2-8 shows an example of a journey map for planning a vacation.

Note   Detailed guidance on the practice of journey mapping and story mapping is beyond the scope of this book but is included because of the important role it plays in developing a shared understanding of the requirements for a software application.

The journey mapping activity can involve user motivations and activities beyond just using the software so that everyone on the team can see and understand the role the desired software plays in the whole narrative. A big part of this is everyone on the team developing empathy for the end-user and clearly articulating the context that the software will be operating in.

---

[6]www.nngroup.com/articles/journey-mapping-101/

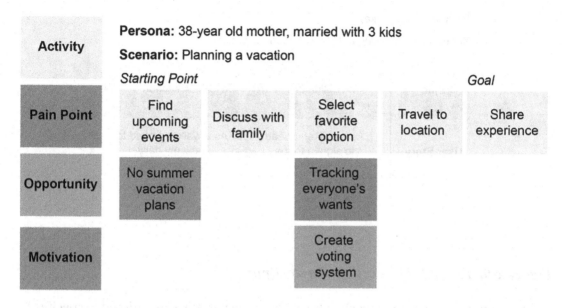

Figure 2-8. *Example of a portion of a journey map*

This process of co-creation proceeds from more of the narrative flow of a journey map to building out user stories and epics using a technique developed by Jeff Patton called story mapping.[7] A story map helps organize the story development. Stories can be located and prioritized within a high-level narrative flow of the user progressing through the software workflow. The goal is to ensure that the entire team maintains the big picture of the overall objectives while working on the details of the stories that make up the project. Figure 2-9 shows an example of part of a story map for a dog walking service.

---

[7]`www.jpattonassociates.com/user-story-mapping/`

Persona: Dog walker

Scenario: Performing a daily walk with multiple dogs

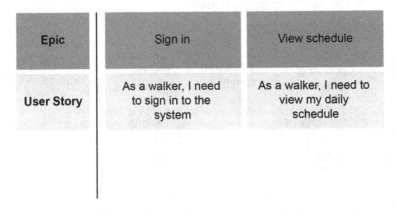

Figure 2-9. *Example of a portion of a story map*

The detailed stories under each of the steps in the narrative are ordered to specify their priority for development by highlighting which stories are in each planned release.

The visual representation of a journey and story map is a powerful touchstone that the team will use to establish and re-establish their shared understandings.

Using Critical Thought to Decompose Requirements

Once we have a shared understanding of the user journey and a comprehensive backlog of high-level stories and epics, we need to turn our focus to reducing uncertainty within the stories and epics themselves.

There has been much written over the years regarding estimation, challenges with estimation, whether we should be estimating at all, etc. (We are looking at you #NoEstimates!) A lot of energy goes into these conversations. It is easy to understand the pushback against estimation. Too often, estimates are held over the heads of people as a firm commitment. It's like people have forgotten the definition of the word "estimate." I will not try and convince you whether estimation, as it is currently viewed, is right or wrong. The fact is, an effective estimation process can be incredibly valuable and essential to the success of the complex software projects we work on and the effectiveness of our agile/lean approach to product development.

In order to do this, we need to think differently about the desired outcomes of estimation and how valuable estimation can be to improve and inform the quality of system design and reduce the uncertainty when trying to determine what should be built. I will make the argument here that estimates are an essential tool for reducing uncertainty and developing a shared understanding. You will think differently about the process and benefits of estimating when we are done.

How Other Engineers Tackle Big Problems

We have a saying at Don't Panic Labs, "the software design process starts with analysis and estimation of the backlog of stories for a project." Most people would not think about estimation as a software design tool, but we do. Much like other engineering disciplines that tackle big and seemingly unsolvable problems by breaking them into smaller solvable problems, we can use analysis and estimation of user stories to arrive at a more "solvable problem." In Andy Weir's novel, *The Martian*, Mark Watney, the main character, was stranded on Mars, and no one knew he was there. His ultimate goal was to get off the planet, but he realized that was not a problem he could attack directly. He analyzed what had to happen to get off the planet as a series of individual problems, and then he began solving all of these smaller problems, starting with growing enough food to survive long enough to be rescued.

When we are provided with a backlog, we are often given epics/stories that may seem quite large and "unsolvable." An example might be, "use computer vision to determine whether a patient is sitting up in bed." That seems daunting, but when you start breaking this down into smaller problems, it starts to feel more manageable.

In this case, it might look like this:

1. Identify the bed in the room

2. Determine if the bed contains a patient

3. Determine if the bed is flat or inclined

4. Determine if there is a person-shaped entity that is in a certain orientation relative to the incline of the bed

This example may seem unusually large in scope (and we would agree), but we use it to illustrate the benefit of breaking bigger problems into smaller ones. Even though we tend to overlook details in bigger problems, as the problems get smaller, we get better at seeing around corners and in the cracks to uncover questions that need answers.

Here's an example of a user story we might be more likely to see: "As a customer, I want to process an order using a credit card for payment." We will call this the "Submit Order" story and use this story to walk through estimation and task decomposition to help gain a shared understanding of the true requirements and reveal uncertainty and any hidden assumptions. But first, let's talk about estimation scales and why they are an important part of this process.

Estimation Scales

Unlike the problems Mark Watney faced, software problems tend to be fairly abstract. This makes it difficult to simply decompose them into smaller problems and be confident that we have done a good job uncovering the details. We need something to help guide us and give us confidence that we have broken down a problem sufficiently enough that we are confident in our understanding. This is where estimation plays a key role and where estimation scales help us stay focused on reducing uncertainty.

An estimations scale is a finite number of choices that we can make when performing estimations. For example, when we are estimating stories in a backlog, we use the following estimation scale:

- 0 effort (uncommon)

- 1/2 a day

- 1 day

- 1/2 a week

- 1 week

- >1 week

We use an estimation scale for a couple of reasons. First, it reinforces that we are estimating by removing the tendency to "put too fine a point" on our estimation by trying to get to the exact number of hours it will take. Estimates are not meant to be precise, so let's not pretend they are.

Second, we believe it is easier for an engineer to assess a relative size of effort using these buckets – even with uncertainty. Relatively small stories (i.e., stories < 1 week) are usually easy to assess in terms of which bucket something will fall into. We often hear comments like, "I think this is probably more than a day, but I don't think it will take 1/2 a week." In this case, we put the estimate at 1/2 week and trust that the Law of Large Numbers[8] will even it out across all estimates – which they almost always do.

---

[8]https://en.wikipedia.org/wiki/Law_of_large_numbers

If we are given a large story that we estimate might take one month to complete, experience tells us we are overlooking a lot of complexity, with the actual effort taking maybe double or triple the estimate. That would be a significant miss and will almost certainly throw other planning and commitments into chaos. By comparison, if you were to decompose that one-month story into smaller stories, each with estimates of a week or less, you might end up with an aggregate estimate of two months that is likely not going to be off by more than a week or two in either direction when compared to the actual effort.

Important   If we are going to make estimates, we owe it to ourselves and our stakeholders to provide an estimate with some degree of accuracy. Making large estimates for stories (e.g., "a month") does not provide a level of accuracy that would make it useful for any real planning or scheduling.

Estimating Our "Submit Order" Story

We favor one-week iterations at Don't Panic Labs. This forces us to "take small bites when eating the elephant." It increases the frequency of delivery to QA and customers for feedback and means we are – at most – one week away from seeing that we might have some schedule risk due to a bad estimate. We have tailored our iteration planning process to be very light, so the one-week rhythm remains efficient with little/no overhead.

Even if we were not on one-week sprint cycles, we would still require all of our stories to have an estimate of one week or less. This is key to helping reveal the uncertainty and hidden assumptions. If we originally think the "Submit Order" story will take two weeks of effort, then it's a safe bet there is a significant amount of uncertainty there. Following our process, we will ask the team (usually an engineer, project manager, and product owner) to decompose the story and estimate the sub-stories that are identified. They will do this until all of the sub-stories are equal to one week or less. For our "Submit Order" story, we might end up with the following:

- As a customer, I want to process an order using a credit card for payment – 2 weeks

- Process credit card authorization – 1 week

- Store order details – 1/2 week

- Verify shopping cart pricing, tax, and shipping – 1/2 week
- Send notification to customer and seller – 1/2 week

Important   This story decomposition and estimation is happening prior to development. The goal of this exercise is to reveal the complexity and hidden assumptions, which is something we want to do *before* we start development. Once we get into traditional sprint planning and development, there will be an additional opportunity to break down the stories into development tasks and provide additional estimates.

The more detailed estimates of the sub-stories add up to about two and a half weeks, which we have much more confidence in than the original two-week estimate for the more abstract original story. We can also see from the story decomposition that there must have been some discussion about the desire to verify the product pricing before submitting the order (rather than just accepting the pricing from the shopping cart). This is a requirement that might not have been articulated in the original description of the main story.

Note   Estimation triangulation is a valuable technique to help with further uncovering details. An example would be to have two separate groups estimate the sub-stories independently and then compare the estimates. This will lead to conversations that will reveal the different assumptions individuals have made about the stories.

As we mentioned in Chapter 1, the outcomes we desire do not fit discretely in a single phase of development. Developing a shared understanding does not end here. In the next chapter, we will discuss some additional tools to uncover incomplete pictures and hidden assumptions when designing the user experience and begin the actual development phases and sprint cycles.

Summary

The hidden productivity vampire for development teams is rework. Most teams do not track this, but what data we have indicates that many teams spend as much as 50% or more of their time on rework. The benefit of reducing this is easy to quantify. A four-person team that reduces their rework from 50% to 25% has effectively added another developer and increased their capacity for feature development by 50%.

Our experience also shows us that one of the best ways to reduce rework is to improve our shared understanding of the system's requirements before we start development. This is going to take more than simply having conversations. It will take a more structured approach designed to reveal complexity and hidden assumptions. It is critical for development teams to engage in analysis and design early in the project cycle, ideally as early as backlog development. This critical thinking will uncover details that were not originally understood.

Journey mapping and story mapping are essential tools for developing a complete representation of the story backlog and the context in which these stories exist. It becomes a physical manifestation of the mental model that is shared by everyone on the team.

Estimation is a powerful tool for telling us how well we truly understand what is involved for a particular story and for uncovering details. Stories that are greater than a week – let alone stories with estimates of a month or more – almost certainly have a lot of unseen details that could disrupt development efforts and plans if they are not discovered until the development phase of the project.

Key Takeaways

- **Rework is a significant drain on productivity for most teams,** and its reduction should be an area of focus.

- **A significant source of rework is a lack of shared understanding** between stakeholders and the development team.

- The larger our teams get, the more likely there are communication challenges and a lack of shared understanding.

- **Conversations alone are a poor means of developing a shared understanding.**

- **Most requirements are knowable before development starts**. Deferring critical thought on requirements until development will increase rework.

- **Structured thought processes and tools enable critical thinking** that reveals hidden assumptions we make about the nature and complexity of a problem and provide an artifact that can be shared among stakeholders for feedback and validation.

- **The best approach to revealing complexity and uncertainty** is to use the age-old process of breaking bigger problems into smaller problems.

- **Estimation is a valuable tool for decomposing bigger problems** and revealing uncertainty and complexity.

Now that we understand how to mitigate the risk and uncertainty leading into a project, we turn our attention to dealing with the challenges, complexity, and uncertainty around the most volatile aspect of modern software applications – the user interface.

CHAPTER 3

Validation of User Experience

Introduction

What is your favorite movie? Is it a Steven Spielberg action flick? Is it a Nora Ephron romantic comedy? How often have we seen reviews from professional movie critics that either applauded a film or gave it a negative review, but then the commercial success of the film is quite the opposite of the reviews? We like certain films because there are things in them that speak to us. And to that end, we are all critics. We all have opinions on the films we watch. We also have opinions about the software we consume. You probably have software you like and software you hate to use, even if you can't explain why. In this chapter, we will focus on what we can do to reduce the volatility (and subsequent rework) in the design and development of user interfaces.

The Evolution of UI Design

Software's user interface (UI) is often the piece of the software most judged. It is also the part of the software system with the largest dependency on approval and acceptance by people not directly involved in the design and development of the system (i.e., the end-users). In the end, it won't matter what the "professional critics" (i.e., the interaction designers) say about the quality of the UI of a piece of software. The only thing that matters is whether it appeals to the target end-user audience. If it does not work for them, then it will not be used. The project will be a failure.

© Doug Durham and Chad Michel 2021
D. Durham and C. Michel, *Lean Software Systems Engineering for Developers*,
https://doi.org/10.1007/978-1-4842-6933-6_3

Complicating this is the fact that the UIs being developed today are increasingly complex as they try to address more complex problems and increase usability. In the 1990s and 2000s, user experience was usually designed by developers. Developers were told to build a screen. They might get some notes describing the fields that need to exist on the UI, but decisions about the actual layout and page behaviors would be largely left to the developer.

Back then, having developers design the UI did have a few advantages. First, developers that liked UI tended to do more UI, so people got to do what they liked. Increasing the happiness of everyone was usually good. Second, since the developers were designing the UI, changes to the designs could be discussed quickly and with good estimates for how long they would take to implement. Third, there are now many seasoned developers out there that have more experience designing UI than they would admit. They are filled with deep knowledge and good instincts on the construction of user experiences.

At some point, specialization made sense. This work was too critical and required the use of different tools to be effective. For example, designing a UI in Microsoft's Visual Studio wasn't as fast as designing it in Adobe's Illustrator. Quickly drawing a UI in a drawing tool to get feedback was going to be more effective than building the entire UI in the actual development environments. Eventually, a new role began to emerge within development teams that focused on designing effective user experiences.

Today user experiences are often designed with tools made specifically for UI. These tools also allow you to test the UI with users. These tools are very different than the development environment tools, such as Visual Studio.

Challenges with Modern UI Design

Given the increasing focus on UI, user experience designers (or user interface designers or user interaction designers) have one of the most difficult jobs in all of software. First, they must design for expert consumers of their work. Second, in today's agile world, they are often told that designing for the experts will take too long, so they must find technically feasible alternatives. Third, completing the UI design is usually a predecessor to planning the development work schedule. This means the rest of the team is actively waiting for the UI work to be done before they can start development. This can be a very tough environment. People that can do this job are some of the most valuable members of a team.

UI matters to everyone, and it is way too important to leave its design to chance. Everyone is an expert, and it is hugely impactful to the success of your application. The increased complexity in the UI can be a large source of rework when building applications. The design of the user experience also affects accessibility by people with disabilities. Having more accessible software enables a larger audience to use it.

Since UI matters so much, we need to ensure we have great user experiences in our applications. How can we ensure that our UI meets the requirements and passes our product owner's approval? For one, we need to reduce as much uncertainty in the UI design as early as possible, by validating its desirability and end-user acceptance before we start development. We can also modify our development strategy to increase the possibility of getting user feedback on the actual working UI long before completing the project. Let's first dive deeper into some of the challenges surrounding UI development in modern systems by using a couple of fictional scenarios. We will follow with a review of a strategy to help reduce the rework that often occurs in the UI as a result of the challenges discussed in the scenarios.

The two scenarios discuss two different categories of challenges when building user experiences. Both experiences should feel realistic. There is a good chance you have experienced similar scenarios yourself.

Scenario 1: Technology

In this first scenario, we will follow the story of a small development team. The team wanted to develop a product that is an "Uber for dog walking." The backlog came together quickly. They created 20 well-formed stories that reasonably represented their product vision.

They engaged their three-person development team to create this new system. After their first agile sprint, they came together to see how everything was going. Each developer chose a different technology path for their work. After the demo, they discussed how the work went. They used two different Microsoft technologies for the system and realized that using two different technologies in a single web application might be a bad choice. They debated between using a legacy technology and a more modern technology based upon model-view-controller pattern (MVC). They liked that the MVC technology is more modern and that Microsoft planned to support this technology for a while. The worry of being stuck on a legacy technology was enough to convince everyone that MVC was the way to go.

They developed much of their user experience successfully using MVC. It worked great for them. There were many good examples on the web for them to reference, and it wasn't that complicated. Unfortunately, MVC wasn't capable of building some of the more complex UI screens they needed for their system. They would have to use some form of JavaScript framework to pull it off and found one that would help them with some of these advanced screens. Implementing those screens using the framework went well.

Now the rest of the application just felt a little clunky. They wanted to bring the rich user experience to the rest of the screens, but just using their JavaScript framework on all the screens seemed short-sighted because it was designed primarily for data binding to the web controls. They decided that what they probably needed was a single-page application (SPA) framework. They did a little looking around, and they found a SPA framework they liked.

They rebuilt much of the system using the SPA framework, which allowed for a more dynamic and engaging user experience. When they completed the rewrite, their CEO gave a new direction to the project: it needs to support a mobile phone experience. After looking at the required changes, they realized they had picked the wrong SPA framework to be successful with the new mobile directive from the CEO.

Constraints of the Modern Web Frameworks

The first story seems almost comical with how many technologies they went through. We have seen worse, including one company that selected four different UI technologies in less than three months. These changes in direction occurred while developers were working on the project. Imagine the churn and frustration of the developers!

Constantly changing UI frameworks seems like a crazy thing to do. Almost unbelievable, but it happens. Teams bounce between Angular, to React, to Vue with no regard for deadlines or product goals. Each framework seems great, and developers argue with almost religious fervor. You will meet developers that will argue strongly for a particular framework only to find out they have never actually shipped a product in the framework.

Now, it seems easy to blame the people making these decisions or to blame the people wanting to change the framework. Remember, everyone cares a lot about the user experience. The bigger problem is that all current web frameworks have limitations and constraints in how they function, the developer experience, and what they will require a developer to do to use that framework to solve the business problem. In general, the UI layer (especially web UIs) is not as mature a development environment as the so-called back-end programming environments. Using a web framework requires compromise and trade-offs. Sometimes these compromises are significant.

When writing the back-end code, the compromises tend to be smaller and more manageable. You might have to trade off asynchronous processing vs. a fully queued framework. Maybe the technology requires you to manually set up your mocking of external services. But these minor issues can usually be worked around in a straightforward way. You can choose one of several popular modern high-order languages or tools for doing back-end development with confidence that you will not be making a decision you will later regret. If you don't keep changing your mind, you can arrive in the realm of "good enough" pretty quickly.

The limitations and constraints are larger with user interface frameworks. We often make trade-offs with front-end development we never would make with back-end development. An example would be automated tests. With back-end development, it would be uncommon to be using a modern back-end programming technology that did not support some form of automated testing. We might need to put in some effort to mock out parts of it, but we would assume we can and should test it using automated tests. We tend to lower our standards and expectations when it comes to client-side, or front-end, technology and developer experience. We would probably assume we *can't* write an automated test against our front-end code or decide it isn't worth the significant effort and time to do it. Testing front-end frameworks is a prime example of the contrast in maturity between back-end development and front-end development.

With user interface frameworks, it isn't just about the JavaScript (or TypeScript) code that lives on the page. It is about the actual visual elements too. The HTML/CSS can be a huge piece of that puzzle. When building modern systems, we usually start with a framework that abstracts the work required to get modern-looking controls on a web page. An example would be Bootstrap, which provides a set of common controls. But those controls are never complete enough, and developers end up having to hand-build some controls on their own to complement the ones they received from their presentation framework. You will be in much better shape when developing your user interface if you can decide early on whether you can live within the box of a given framework. When everything is possible, any designer will select options that may or may not be feasible within the constraints of the chosen technology. Ensuring that the UI designer understands what is and what is not possible within the chosen UI framework will reduce their solution search space and ensure you are building *in* your framework and not just *on* your framework.

Business Logic Bleeding into the UI Layer

Every time the team chose a new technology, they ended up with a lot of rework. It started with the first sprint when they reimplemented their work in MVC, instead of continuing development in the legacy technology. This rework continued with each new technology they chose. But how *much* rework was it?

A big factor would be how much of their business logic and user workflow orchestration resides in the client layer. The more logic/workflow that is in the client tier, the more rework you will need to do with each technology change.

One good thing about using older legacy technologies is that, in general, it was harder to let a lot of business logic bleed into the client tier. As we have moved to modern web frameworks, it has become more and more common to put a large portion of the business logic into the client layer. It is appealing to do this, but as master architect Juval Löwy points out,[1] our applications are more likely to change in the client tier than in a back-end service (see Figure 3-1). Our systems change over time, and that is a natural and good thing. It is an indicator of a system that is being used. We have seen that those changes tend to be greater in the presentation/client layer than in the business logic layer. It makes sense that our UI has the highest frequency of change as this is where end-user preferences and feedback on screens and behaviors tend to be focused.

As a result, the more business logic is packed into the UI layer, the more likely it is that the business logic will have to change. In our previous scenario, if they kept the business logic on the server, that would have greatly reduced the amount they would have to reimplement with each technology change.

---

[1]Löwy, Juval. 2020. *Righting Software*. Addison-Wesley Professional.

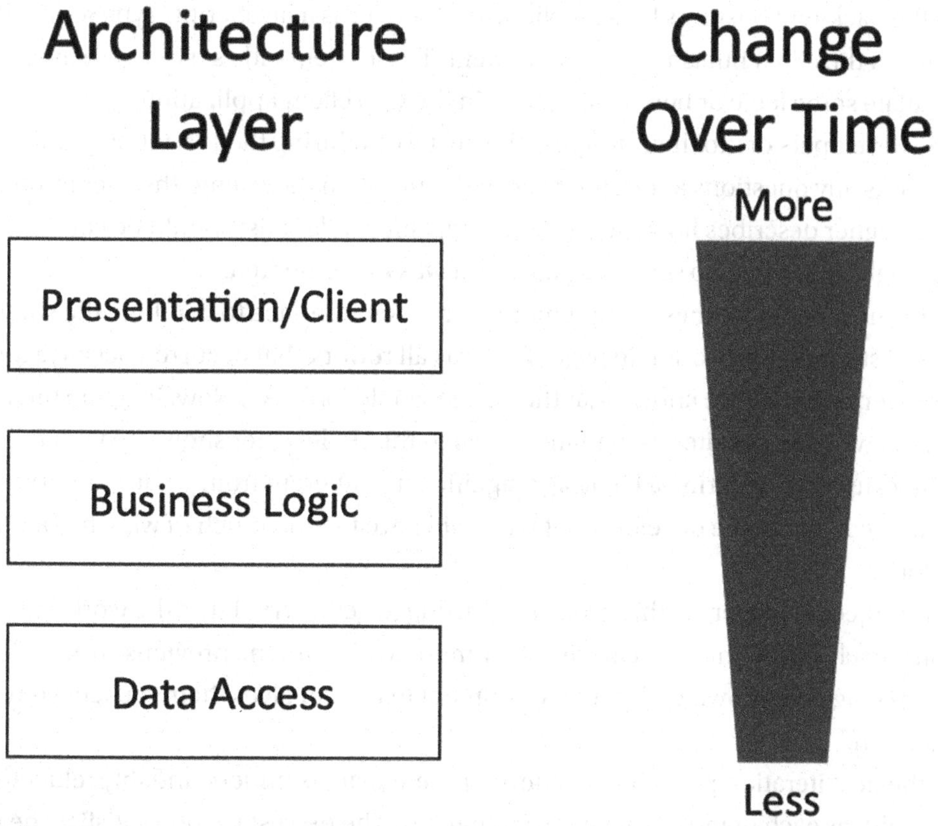

Architecture Layer

Change Over Time

More

Presentation/Client

Business Logic

Data Access

Less

Figure 3-1. *Frequency of change decreases as you move down the stack*

Scenario 2: Process

Our second story of UI development is less about the technology and more about the process. Imagine we have a different company being asked to build a dashboard to display student grade data. This dashboard needs to display student information in an aggregate and also down to an individual student level. The team created their backlog for this dashboard. They quickly got through the creation of their 30 stories in a long whiteboard meeting. After the meeting, they realized they needed some work for the developers while the UI was being designed. The development team started working on some stories using the notes and conversations from the whiteboard session.

The database and back-end code came together quickly. The user interface was off to a pretty good start, too. They set up a new web project to display this information. They created a student list component and a student detail component to display the data as discussed during the backlog creation meeting. And they created a client-side service to call the back-end business logic. A client-side service is a JavaScript/TypeScript class that runs in the client but isn't a UI component. These client-side services are used to encapsulate some logic or behavior needed in the web client application.

The developers demo their progress the next week during their iteration planning. No one asks any questions about the back end. But, when they demo the user interface, the UI designer describes how the student detail and student list should be combined onto a single page, not two separate pages as it was implemented.

In the next iteration, they reimplemented the user interface to combine the student detail and student list on a single page. This was all rework that occurred because the development team didn't know what the design would look like. Now, imagine their frustration with the next iteration planning when the UI designer shows up with full-color mockups that describe a UI design significantly different from what was currently implemented. Again, the development team will have to redo much of what has already been done.

The project manager for this project is starting to get worried that the work will never get done. Each sprint, they are carrying over more work from the previous sprint. The project manager sits down with the development team and gives them the "get your stuff done speech."

At the next iteration planning, the development team is understandably reluctant to demo again, as each demo has resulted in changes. The newest version satisfies the user interface designer's goal of having the student details and student list pages be the same page. But the product owner shows up for this meeting and points out that they need to have the student details available as a stand-alone page.

At this point, the development team would be extremely frustrated. How many times could they be asked to redo something? As a rule, software developers do not enjoy rework; developers enjoy plowing ahead and creating new software.

Not everything about this process was a disaster. The fact that the UI designer was reviewing the work is excellent. Having an engaged product owner is also essential to the success of a software project. Getting feedback from a product owner before end-users see the user interface is a "must-have" practice. Nevertheless, there were some significant issues that resulted in a lot of rework. It is important to ask why.

Missing Artifacts

Many mistakes were made in this scenario. The first might be the most obvious. An experienced developer will point out that development started before the UI design was complete. This may be obvious, but it remains a common problem with many development projects. Why is it that user interface designs often come in after the developers already have a lot of the work done?

Any type of design process is usually iterative, with each iteration providing more details. For some reason, when we design user experiences, we often don't have a hand-off between designers and developers until the user experience is at a full, final mockup level. This takes time and often leads to development teams pushing forward without these designs.

The development team could have made better-informed decisions if they had access to less-polished wireframes that showed the page interactions and the general flow of the site. This intermediate step would have helped the development team instead of waiting until the user interface designer was fully done with the polished, high-fidelity mockups. These intermediate, lower fidelity designs would have helped keep the developer consistent with the final design and could have been reviewed by the product owner to avoid the "where did my page go" moment from the last meeting.

Like with any design, we need to make multiple passes and multiple artifacts to express it in its entirety. For UI designs, there are three key artifacts that developers need, as described in Table 3-1. We will show examples of these artifacts in the last part of this chapter.

Table 3-1. *Key artifacts of the UI design process*

Artifact	Description
Screen Flow	Screen flows show the flow of how the screens interact. This interaction of the screens should be done early and can be done in a low-fidelity way.
Wireframe	Wireframes capture the essence of a screen but are not picture-perfect. They can often be done in grayscale and capture a lot of what will be on a screen and how it will function, but won't provide pixel-level details to the developer.
Mockup	The term mockup refers to something like an exact picture of the user interface, as it would be built by the software developer. These full-color pictures are close to an exact blueprint for how the UI should look at a given screen size.

Note   Continuing with our analogy about building a house, a wireframe is roughly equivalent to the initial drawings an architect might make for a house that show the general layout of the rooms and how the house might look from the outside so that the customer can get a feel for the concept and what changes would be required before doing more detailed design. A mockup would then be equivalent to the detailed plan and elevation views that the architect would create that would show detailed dimensions of rooms, visual and aesthetic details, and materials used for exterior and interior parts of the house.

We should never just jump straight to full-color mockups. Full-color mockups take more time to create than do wireframes and screen flows. The irony here is that screen flows often provide some of the most useful information about user experience and are often omitted completely. In most systems, full-color mockups are only needed for a few key screens. You can get away with wireframes for most of the screens in an application.

No Accommodation for UI Design Time

The second problem is one of planning. We need to plan out our projects so we know when we will need designs for UI screens. We can't be in a meeting designing the requirements and expect to have mockups, wireframes, or screen flows to immediately be ready for the developer. The user interface team needs time to do the design and create these artifacts. We need to be in front of these requests, and the UI needs to be operating at least a few sprints ahead of the developers. User interfaces take time, and because they are so essential, we should give them the time needed to be developed. Because all following work is dependent on the UI, the UI must be completed on schedule. This requires realistic expectations of when it can be done.

Failure to Communicate

The third problem occurs when the developer does not ask enough questions and makes too many assumptions. The developer should have stood outside the user interface designer's door until they had enough information to proceed. If there wasn't enough information to confidently start on this work, the developer needed to raise their hand and get answers. In an ideal world with a mature development team, the project manager and everyone else on the team would also have known that more information was needed.

Strategy for Effective UI Validation

The creation of good user experiences is essential, and as you saw with our scenarios the path to creating good user experiences is potentially problematic. If we leave UI development to chance, we will get a random outcome. Sometimes we will get a good user experience, and sometimes we won't. An organized process for UI design and validation is critical. In this section, we will walk through a sequential workflow for reducing the risk and uncertainty of UI design and development. This workflow contains the following 12 steps:

- Generate good requirements

- Develop acceptance criteria

- Develop screen flow and wireframes

- Review the preliminary UI design

- Develop mockups

- Review the mockups

- Design the UI components

- Define the client/server interactions

- Build the UI using mock data

- Review the working UI

- Integrate working UI with the real back end

Generate Good Requirements

The first stage of a successful UI project is defining good requirements. We need to work as a team to define the high-level requirements for the project. These requirements need to be at least at a story level. The requirements need to be fairly complete, and they must be correct. When defining requirements at this level, it is important to make sure everyone understands the requirements. Thanks to the pervasive adoption of agile methods for requirements management, most modern development teams are effective at developing good requirements.

Develop Acceptance Criteria

The best way to get well-understood requirements is to create acceptance criteria for those requirements. Acceptance criteria should reflect the many scenarios through the software that need to be supported by that requirement. It is recommended to use a structured format, such as the Gherkin language (see Figure 3-2), when writing the stories used to define test cases. This will make them more consistent.

Feature: Submit Order

Scenario: Successful order submission

GIVEN shopper has item in shopping cart
      AND shopping has provided VALID CC information
WHEN shopper submits the order
THEN shopper's order is accepted
      AND shopper taken to order confirmation
      AND email notification sent to shopper
      AND email notification sent to fulfillment center

Scenario: Failed order submission because of bad CC

GIVEN shopper has item in shopping cart
      AND shopping has provided an INVALID CC information
WHEN shopper submits the order
THEN shopper's order is denied
      AND shopper receives an error regarding CC

Scenario: Failed order submission because out of stock

GIVEN shopper has item in shopping cart
      AND shopper has provided a VALID CC information
      AND cart item is out of stock
WHEN shopper submits the order
THEN shopper's order is denied
      AND shopper receives an error about out of stock

Figure 3-2. Acceptance criteria for an ecommerce Submit Order story

Develop Screen Flows and Wireframes

The next step recommended is screen-flowing the system (see Figure 3-3). This step could be done after creating wireframes (see Figure 3-4), but it is recommended you create both before building mockups. The screen flow and wireframes should be low-fidelity and built quickly. A common problem with your projects is the lack of definition early. The sooner everyone can look at something that represents the UI look and flow, the sooner we will uncover hidden assumptions and reduce uncertainty. The screen flow and wireframes can be done in parallel with the creation of the acceptance criteria. It is recommended to do the acceptance criteria first, but they can be done in parallel.

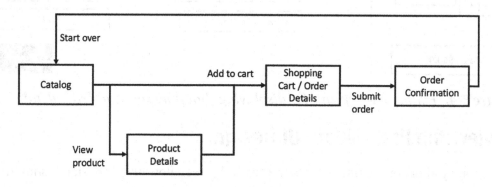

***Figure 3-3.** Example screen flow for the Submit Order story*

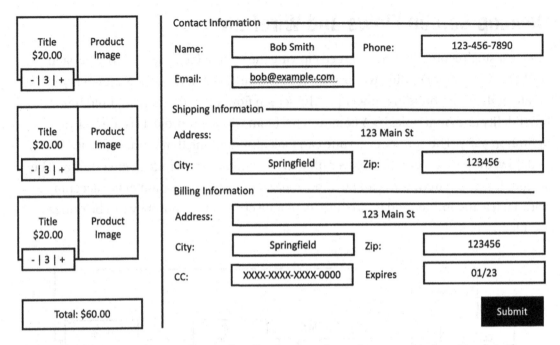

Figure 3-4. *Example wireframe for displaying shopping cart and order details*

Review the Preliminary UI Design

Immediately after completing the wireframes and screen flow, the UI designer should have a meeting with the stakeholders and developers to review the wireframes and screen flows created. This would be an informal meeting where everyone can ask questions to ensure they understand the UI. Everyone should be asking, "can these designs accommodate the requirements?" Since we are not looking at individual controls or styles, our focus will be more on the flow of the application at this point.

Develop Mockups

Once the wireframes and screen flow pass the design review, mockups (see Figure 3-5) should be built out. Not every screen typically will need to have a mockup. The key and most important screens should have mockups to demonstrate the intended design to the developers.

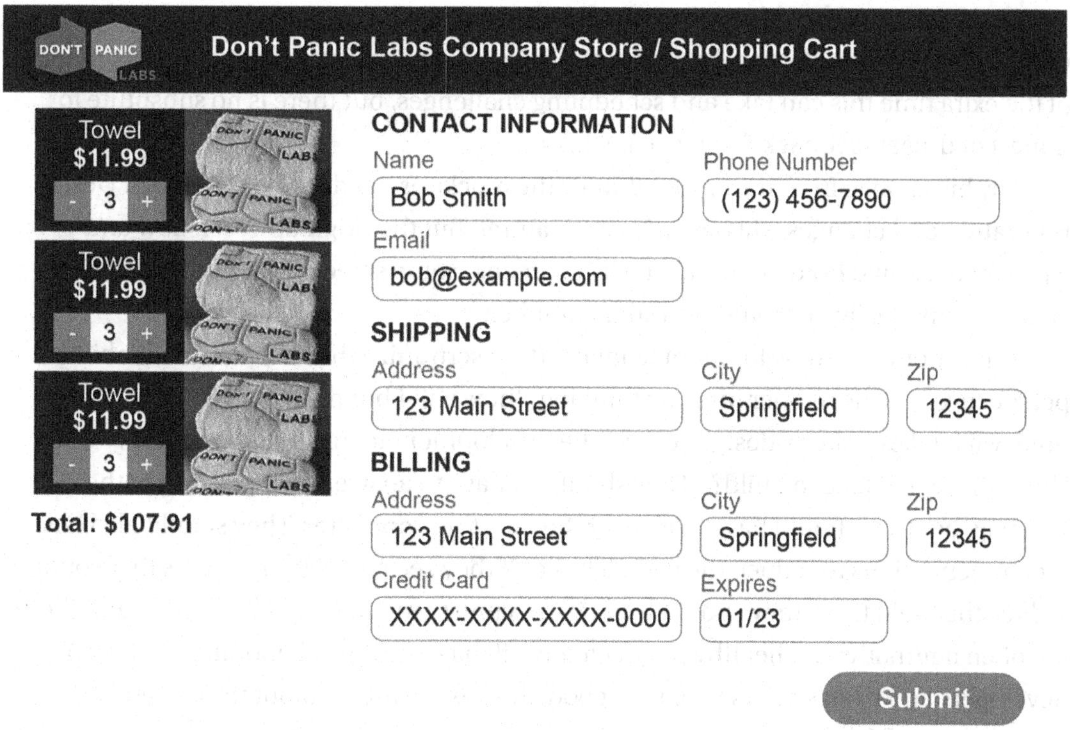

Figure 3-5. *Example mockup for the shopping cart and order details screen*

This brings us to an important point; this phase must be done in collaboration with developers. Ideally, the UI designer and the development lead will work closely during this phase. As the UI designer decides on a particular UI concept for a control, the development lead should verify that the intended framework will support that control. If there is any doubt, the development lead should quickly standup a separate application to demonstrate that the framework's control can do what is intended. We call this a UI spike. As we discussed earlier, you can save a significant amount of effort on any UI project if the design is easily supported by the UI framework that will be used. Only violate this rule if it is essential for the success of the project.

Review the Mockups

The next activity is a design review for the mockups. All project stakeholders (product owner, project manager, the developers, and the UI team) should be involved. Everyone needs to be scrutinizing the design. Remember, everyone is an expert consumer of UI, so everyone's opinion matters.

Design reviews should involve actual end-users, not just the product owner, but people who will actually use the software. Using real end-users is often skipped because of the extra time this can take and scheduling challenges, but there is no substitute for honest end-user feedback if you can get it.

Any big change from the screen flow or the mockups needs to be explained. Design is iterative, and changes will occur. That is natural. But the original screen flow and wireframes should hold up for most of the screens. Some screens will need significant changes, but ideally, it should be a small number.

At this point, the development team needs to scrutinize the UI from a buildability perspective. The developer must be thinking, "how will I build this?" and "how much time will it take?" After a design review, the development team should be asked, "how long will it take to build?" They shouldn't have to answer that question in the meeting, but they should have to answer the question soon after. They should also have recommendations to reduce the overall build. If they see controls or options that could reduce the build time, they should bring it up. Time to market and cost matter, and there are often alternatives. A healthy project team will have strong collaboration between developers and UI designers to ensure good choices are made about the design and construction of the UI.

Another perspective that must be included in this design review is accessibility. The UI designer must explain how the application will handle accessibility for all users. We want software that is easy to use for all users. Catching these accessibility issues early is way easier than after the application has been built. Not only is accessibility good for business, but these accessibility requirements are often legal requirements.

The following are key considerations and questions to be covered during the mockup review:

- Mockups show enough of the UI for developers

- Mockups match the wireframes/screen flows

  - Do the wireframe and screen flows need updating?

- Mockups clearly describe how they will make the software accessible

- Mockups meet the branding/product requirements

- Build considerations…

- All control usage is documented

- Any custom controls are documented

- Do we need to do a prototype for any custom controls?

- Everyone understands how these screens will facilitate the requirements

Design the UI Components

Once we have the mockups, we can begin designing the individual components we will use to build the user interface. Ideally, we would take each mockup/wireframe and break it down into components (see Figure 3-6). This work can be done before the mockup phase, or this work can start after the wireframe/screen flow phase. It is best to start this after the mockup phase if you can. If you start this work early against the wireframes/screen flow, you will need to come back and update the design after the mockup review.

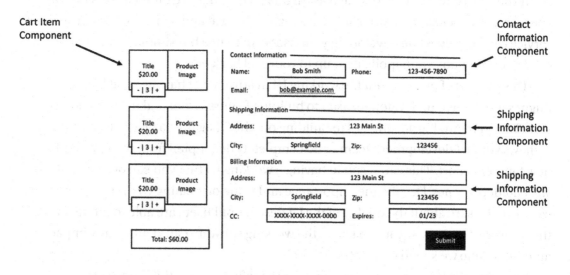

Figure 3-6. *Components for the submit order screen*

The component design needs to cover all screens. Each component used to build that UI needs to be called out. If you are using a framework like Angular, each client-side service should also be called out.

Define the Client/Server Interactions

After designing the UI components, you should define the interaction between the client and the server. This could be done graphically using interaction diagrams and data contract or DTO (Data Transfer Object) definitions, or it could be a simple document with API methods and data descriptions. The exact way you express this part of the design will vary from project to project. The key is to think through this before starting construction so that you are working from a plan instead of making these decisions on the fly.

Build the UI Using Mock Data

Once you have your data contracts and client/server interactions defined, you can begin building your application. This should initially be done against mock data (representing the back-end interactions) that lives completely in your client tier.

If you are using a framework such as Angular,[2] you can have different versions of your services. For example, you can have a regular service and a mock service. The mock service can be used while developing your user experience but should be maintained even after you hook your application up to your real back end.

This process of building out the working UI in advance of having a real back end might seem foreign to developers used to building features front end to back end in one step. There are two big advantages to building out the UI against a fake back end. First, it allows your UI development team to be completely decoupled from the back-end development effort. This can result in having a working UI that you can demonstrate to stakeholders sooner. Despite the importance and value of creating UI design artifacts, we can never be sure about the quality of the UI design until users are able to interact with the software. Getting early feedback on the working software can significantly impact the amount of time we spend on rework.

The second advantage is that it allows for the refinement of the client/server interactions and data contracts that will always occur as we start building the UI. Refining this API between the client and the server before we start back-end development reduces the possibility of rework on the back end.

---

[2]https://angular.io

Review the Working UI

After you have your UI stood up against fake data, you should have the UI team review the working software. This review can look at what is built from a variety of perspectives and ensure that we are building what is expected.

Ideally, this review should not wait until all of the UI is stood up. After each screen (or group of screens) is implemented, put it in front of the UI team. Make sure they are confident you are implementing what is expected. Again, the sooner we realize we are off the path, the better.

Another key member of this UI review is the product owner. The product owner should also look at the UI running against fake data with a critical eye and ensure the software will meet the goals of the product.

The following are key considerations and questions to be covered during the review of the working UI:

- UI matches mockups, wireframes, and screen flow

- UI performance is acceptable

- UI meets accessibility requirements

- UI is using the correct controls and frameworks as defined earlier

- UI is usable. You can use the UI to achieve acceptance criteria

Integrate Working UI with the Real Back End

Last, we have to wire up the UI against the real back end. At this point, the work should be a rewriting of a single client-side service to call a back end. Hopefully, the back end is already in place at this point, making this just a matter of getting the wires connected.

Summary

UI complexity and sophistication have sky-rocketed since the early 2000s. The user experience can often make or break a product, so getting the user experience right has become a key priority for most software development projects. Despite this, user experience design and development is an area most often noted for its frustration and challenges unrelated to the design process. Whereas other aspects of software development have seen remarkable improvements in tooling and productivity, developing user experiences still seems to be bogged down in a swamp of frameworks, markup, code, browser compatibilities, testing issues, mobile platforms, and tooling that is still maturing. The result is a significant amount of time being spent developing and stabilizing a user experience compared to other aspects of a software development project.

Building modern UIs is often more complex than building the corresponding back-end code. And yet, when we take on building a user experience, we often miss many important steps to help reduce the amount of rework. Until we bring the productivity of UI development to the level of back-end development, we need to emphasize non-coding activities such as validating designs. This can reduce the amount of time we spend working and reworking the client layer code. This chapter focused on some activities and strategies that can improve your user interface development process.

Key Takeaways

- **A strong user experience can be a significant differentiator with your competition, or it can be a huge boat anchor around your neck.**

- **Make a conscious choice to live within the constraints of a chosen web framework**. Make sure the UI designer understands the controls and capabilities they have to work with so they don't design something that a developer will have to build from scratch.

- **There is an ever-increasing demand for interaction design** due to the types of problems we are trying to solve in software and the variety of end-user devices we are targeting.

- **UI development on any project is the most volatile area, with the most rework and effort.**

- **UI tends to be a dynamic experience and often requires working code to validate with many users.**

- **UI development is not as efficient as back-end development**, which increases the need to minimize rework.

- **Having a strategy/process for prototyping and testing UI concepts prior to development** will reduce uncertainty and increase the shared understanding between stakeholders and the development team.

- **Prioritizing key UI development work over back-end work can reduce overall project rework** by providing more insights into the business logic layer API requirements and help minimize/avoid business logic in the UI layer.

- **Ensuring UI team members are reviewing and testing the development work** will help ensure a successful transition from design to implementation.

With a firm handle on managing the complexity and uncertainty in the user experience, we now turn our attention to how we build back-end systems that enable change throughout their lifetime.

CHAPTER 4

Designing Software Systems That Age Well and Adapt to Change

Introduction

Building systems that are as easy to understand and maintain in year five as they were in year one does not happen naturally. It takes deliberate and disciplined effort, along with a firm grasp of the reasons, to understand why systems become difficult to change. This resistance to change is known as software entropy, which is the natural tendency of software to devolve toward disorder and chaos. In this chapter, we will focus on what it takes to design, build, and maintain systems that age well and can adapt to change over the lifetime of the project.

Reality Check

Take a moment and think back about the reasons you were drawn to software development and why you chose it as a career. I imagine many of you would say something like, "I like solving problems with software" or "it's cool how I can type up something, hit run, and see it working." Some of you might have chosen this career field because you saw it as an opportunity to have a positive impact on people's lives, or maybe you just felt you had a talent, and this would be a way to have some financial security given the demand for these skills. Whatever your reason, it was likely something positive (see Figure 4-1).

© Doug Durham and Chad Michel 2021
D. Durham and C. Michel, *Lean Software Systems Engineering for Developers*,
https://doi.org/10.1007/978-1-4842-6933-6_4

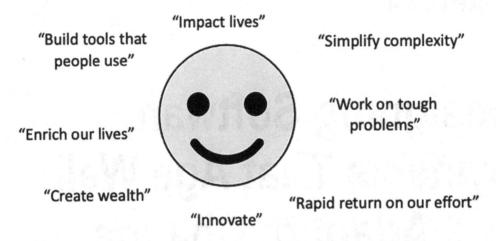

Figure 4-1. *Reasons why we choose to develop software*

Now, I'm sure that none of us expected our jobs to be all sunshine and happiness all the time, but there is an alarming amount of "pain" involved in being in this career field. For many of us, every day can feel like a struggle, and that we are always having to push back or defend ourselves against some new problem, or some perception, or an unrealistic expectation, or a timeline that will be missed. The conversations we are having and hearing are not putting smiles on our faces (see Figure 4-2).

Figure 4-2. *What our experiences are like*

As a result, it can often feel like the things we loathe about our job and career are overshadowing what made us choose this career in the first place (see Figure 4-3). It's almost like our career and our industry are better represented by a big angry face than the happy face we were expecting.

What we enjoy   **What we loathe**

Figure 4-3. *What we are experiencing*

Let's take a hard look at why we are having these negative feelings. We may find that the reasons for these feelings fall into one or both of these categories: (1) the organization we work for is toxic or (2) the software we are working on is a giant mess that is difficult to work in and understand. Dealing with toxic organizations is not within our sphere of influence and control (and it is out of scope for this book, sorry). However, designing and building software that does not become a giant mess is very much in our control and is the focus of this chapter. Building systems that age well is one of the key outcomes that can have a significant impact on shifting the balance between what we loathe in our jobs and what we enjoy (see Figure 4-4).

What we enjoy   **What we loathe**

Figure 4-4. *What we want*

Errors in Judgment Revisited

In Chapter 1, we discussed how this general decay of our systems is a result of errors in judgment. These errors in judgment are symptoms of a deficiency in our systematic, disciplined, and quantifiable approach to software development. We outlined several ways in which these errors in judgment manifest themselves, which we summarize here:

- Making changes becomes more and more difficult.

- Changes made in one part of the system unknowingly create defects in other parts of the system.

- It is challenging for developers to gain an understanding of the system.

- It is easier for a developer to do the wrong thing (violate a design philosophy) than do the right thing.

The goal of this chapter is to introduce a number of concepts and principles related to system design that will reduce these deficiencies in our approach to software development, and as a result decrease our errors in judgment, which impact how well our systems age and adapt to change.

Case Study: Notification Subsystem

We have found it is much easier to illustrate these errors in judgment related to design decisions by exploring concrete examples. To start, let's explore what we would consider a typical scenario by reviewing a fictional case study that demonstrates how these problems can manifest at both an architectural level and in detailed design. Imagine you are part of a development team that works for an ecommerce platform company that sells physical goods online. Your team's responsibility is to build and maintain an Order Notification subsystem that will send confirmation emails when orders are placed. Someone in the organization (presumably an enterprise architect) previously identified the subsystems of this platform, and development teams were formed around these subsystems that are shown in Table 4-1.

Table 4-1. *Subsystem responsibilities for the ecommerce platform*

Subsystem	Responsibility
Order Processing	Responsible for the processing of order requests from customers, including order data creation and payment processing
Order Notification	Responsible for sending order confirmation details to customers
Shopping Cart Management	Responsible for managing and storing the shopping carts that customers create
Customer Profile	Responsible for creating and maintaining customer account information
Order Shipping	Responsible for shipping orders that have been placed

Figure 4-5 lays out these subsystems, and while there might be a better way to break up this large system, what is shown would be considered reasonable by current industry standards.

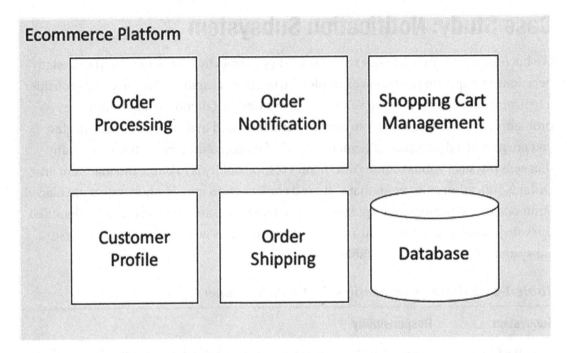

Figure 4-5. *Ecommerce subsystems*

For sending customer order confirmation emails, the Order Processing team will need to send your subsystem some information when an order is successfully placed. Your team coordinates with the Order Processing team and defines an API method titled SendOrderConfirmation. This API takes an email address and an order object that contains the required information to build and send the email. The high-level workflow is shown in Figure 4-6.

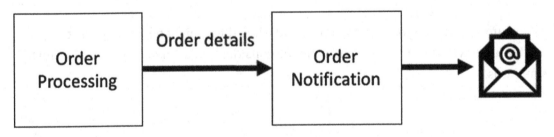

Figure 4-6. *High-level Order Notification workflow*

Listing 4-1 shows the details of this interface definition for the Send Order Confirmation API.

Listing 4-1. Interface with Send Order Confirmation API

```
public interface IMessageSender
{
        void SendOrderConfirmation(string customerEmail,
                            OrderDetails orderDetails);
}
```

Your team works through the details of how you are going to send these emails and come up with the major components of the Order Notification subsystem. Table 4-2 lists these components and their description.

Table 4-2. *Component descriptions for Order Notification subsystem*

Component	Description
Message Sender	This is the main module that orchestrates the sending of the email. This module contains the SendOrderConfirmation method that is used by the Order Processing subsystem.
Message Formatter	The plan for building these emails is to use templates and text merging, so your team decides it would be wise to encapsulate this activity in its own component.
Templates Data Store	The product owner mentioned that they would want to occasionally make modifications to the format of the emails in order to place ads and other messages within them. Your team decides it makes sense to have separate storage for these email templates that will be created.
SMTP Service	The plan is to use the existing internal email system to send out the customer emails.
Configuration	The SMTP API requires some configuration data to be sure we are accessing the production API and not the QA API. These settings will be stored in a configuration file that the Message Sender component will access.

Figure 4-7 shows the details of the order confirmation email workflow.

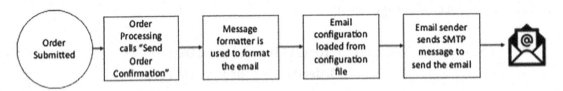

Figure 4-7. *Order Confirmation workflow*

Figure 4-8 shows how the Order Notification subsystem components interact to accomplish this workflow.

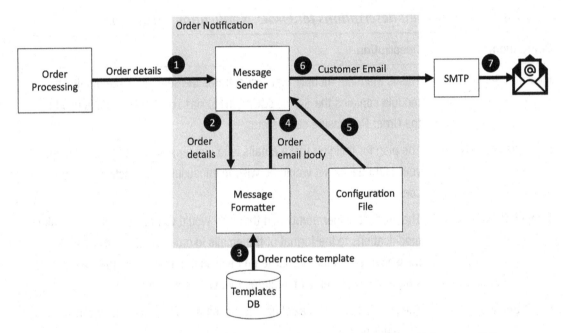

Figure 4-8. *Order Notification subsystem* SendOrderConfirmation *workflow*

Your team develops and deploys the Order Notification subsystem to the integration test environment, and everything is working great. During the retrospective, you discuss how you weren't able to create as many automated tests as you had wanted. It seems like this was a lot tougher than everyone thought it would be. Hopefully, you'll be able to spend more time on this later.

Change 1: Supplier Order Email

During the initial development, the product owner comes to the teams to tell them that some of the goods being sold will be supplied by vendors who will need a separate notification when an order is placed for those items. Your team and the Order Processing team decide the best way to do this is to create an additional API method called SendSupplierOrderNotice, which will be called for each supplier on the order that requires this notification. The Order Processing team will determine which suppliers need this notice and call the API method. Figure 4-9 shows the workflow for this new API.

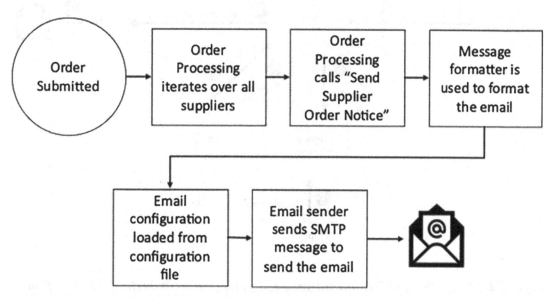

Figure 4-9. *Supplier Order Notice workflow*

Listing 4-2 shows the updated interface definition with the new Send Supplier Order Notice API.

Listing 4-2. Updated interface with the Send Supplier Order Notice API

```
public interface IMessageSender
{
        void SendOrderConfirmation(string customerEmail,
                             OrderDetails orderDetails);
        void SendSupplierOrderNotice(string supplierEmail,
                             OrderDetails orderDetails);
}
```

While this felt like a late change for the version 1 release, both teams were able to accommodate, and the schedule was only slightly adjusted. Your team implements the new email workflow, which requires the new method in the Message Sender module and a new method in the Message Formatter module to handle the supplier email data and new templates. Once again, few tests were created for this new feature. Figure 4-10 shows the supplier order notice workflow.

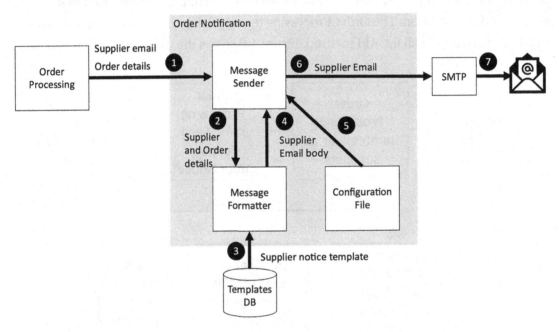

Figure 4-10. *Order Notification subsystem* SendSupplierOrderNotice *workflow*

Change 2: Order Shipped Notices

Shortly after version 1 of the system goes into production, the product owners come back to say they've gotten good feedback on the platform but that they would like to have an email sent when their order has shipped so that the customers can begin tracking its arrival. Everyone agrees this makes sense, so your team and the Order Shipping team begin implementing this feature.

Since this feature feels fairly similar to order confirmation emails, your team suggests that a new API method be created called SendShippingNotice, which contains a shipped order object with everything needed to send the email (similar to

SendOrderConfirmation and SendSupplierOrderNotice). The Shipping team agrees. Figure 4-11 shows the high-level workflow for this new feature. Listing 4-3 shows the updated interface definition with the new Send Shipping Notice API.

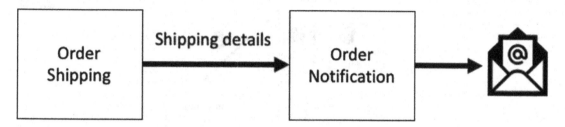

Figure 4-11. *High-level Shipping Notice workflow*

Listing 4-3. Updated interface with the Send Shipping Notice API

```
public interface IMessageSender
{
        void SendOrderConfirmation(string customerEmail,
                      OrderDetails orderDetails);
        void SendSupplierOrderNotice(string supplierEmail,
                      OrderDetails orderDetails);
        void SendShippingNotice(string customerEmail,
                      ShippedOrderDetails shippedOrderDetails);
}
```

Your team implements the new email workflow, which requires the new method in the Message Sender module as well as a new method in the Message Formatter module to handle the shipping email data and new templates. Figure 4-12 shows the shipping notice workflow.

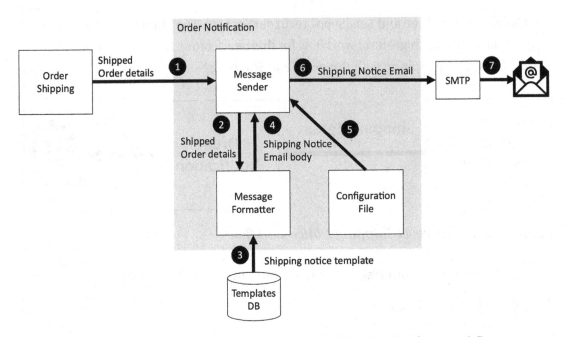

Figure 4-12. *Order Notification subsystem SendShippingNotice workflow*

Change 3: New SMTP Service

Customer support raised a potential issue as a result of the number of inquiries they have been getting from customers saying they never received their order confirmation. Upon further investigation, it appears that the company's email server IP addresses have been blacklisted as potential spam. After a slight panic attack, your team recommends switching to using a third-party email service that actively manages blacklisting. The product owner agrees, and you replace the logic in each of the notification methods with new logic for the Email API and the new API configuration data. Figure 4-13 shows an example of a workflow using the new Email API.

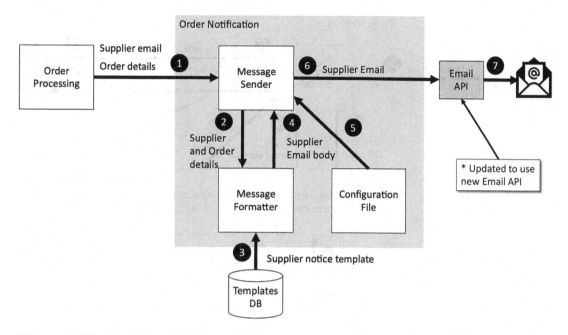

Figure 4-13. *New Email API*

Change 4: Order Notices for Shipping

The internal shipping team learned about the Supplier Order Email and decided they would also like to have more real-time notifications of when orders have been placed that will require shipping. Ideally, this notice would be initiated by the Order Processing subsystem, but that team is very busy implementing some new payment types and would not be able to get to this in time for the next release. During a brainstorming session with your team, it was decided that the shipping department would be happy just to get the standard customer order notices. They would parse the email for the information they needed. This seemed like an easy and expedient solution given the circumstances. The only tricky part was the need to look at the order details to determine if it contained line items that would need to be shipped and only send them an email in that case.

   The scope of changes for this feature required modifying the SendOrderConfirmation method to include the logic that determines whether the order contained shipped items. In that case, when an order is placed, a duplicate customer notification email is sent to the shipping department. This email address for the shipping department is stored in the service's configuration file. This seemed like a good solution to the problem. Figure 4-14 shows the modified customer order notice workflow.

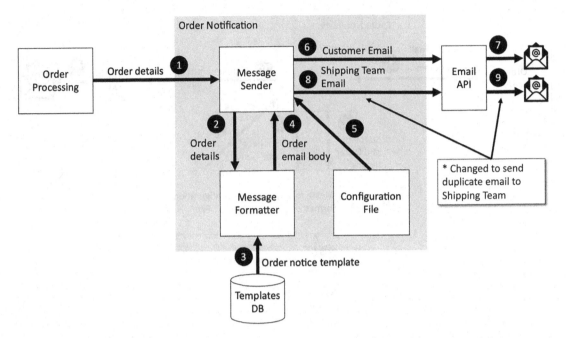

Figure 4-14. *Order Notification subsystem modified* SendOrderConfirmation *workflow*

Change 5: Abandoned Cart Notices

Next, the marketing department has been analyzing the website metrics and has noticed that many customers are putting items in their carts but are not completing the purchase. They want to do something about the high number of these abandoned carts and have decided to send an email to the customers encouraging them to complete their purchase if the cart is abandoned for more than a week. They might even test some uses of discounts or coupons at some point to encourage them.

Your team and the Shopping Cart Management team get together to discuss how to accommodate this feature request. You show them the existing APIs being used by the Order Processing and Order Shipping team. They reluctantly agree to follow the same pattern even though they would prefer to just send your team a simple message and then have you take care of the details. They expect to continue making changes to this feature, and they have a lot of stuff on their plate already. The message idea sounded intriguing to you, but you feel like following the established pattern is a prudent decision.

As a result, you now create a new API method called SendAbandonedCartEmail, which contains a cart object along with everything else needed to send the email. Figure 4-15 shows the high-level workflow for this new feature. Listing 4-4 shows the updated interface definition with the new Send Abandoned Cart Email API.

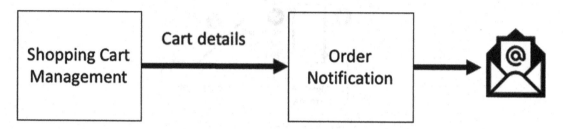

Figure 4-15. *High-level Abandoned Cart Email workflow*

Listing 4-4. Updated interface with the Send Abandoned Cart Email API

```
public interface IMessageSender
{
        void SendOrderConfirmation(string customerEmail,
                        OrderDetails orderDetails);
        void SendSupplierOrderNotice(string supplierEmail,
                        OrderDetails orderDetails);
        void SendShippingNotice(string customerEmail,
                        ShippedOrderDetails shippedOrderDetails);
        void SendAbandonedCartEmail(string customerEmail,
                        CartDetails cartDetails);
}
```

Your team implements the new email workflow, which requires the new method in the Message Sender module as well as a new method in the Message Formatter module to handle the abandoned cart email data and new templates. The Message Sender module is starting to get a lot of code in it but still seems to be holding up to the design. Figure 4-16 shows the abandoned cart notice workflow.

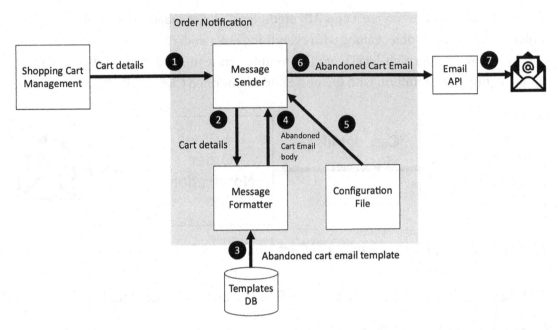

Figure 4-16. *Order Notification subsystem modified* SendAbandonedCartEmail *workflow*

Change 6: The Change That Forces the Redesign Conversations

The feedback from marketing's voice of the customer project revealed a strong preference for customers to have the option to get their notices using methods other than just email. At first, you think this is no big deal, and then you start to realize everything that will have to change to support this. Almost every subsystem has code specific to sending emails to customers. Your immediate response to the product owner is that this will create a lot of work for almost every team. They can't understand why simply sending a text message instead of an email is that big of a deal. You start to go into the details of how everything works, and their eyes start to glaze over. In the end, you are tasked with coming back with the plan and estimates to get this done in the next release.

You gather the leads of the other subsystem teams to discuss the changes that will be required. Table 4-3 lists the results of your analysis.

Table 4-3. *Analysis of changes required to support text messages*

Subsystem	Changes Required
Order Processing	Get communication preference and transport detail information from Customer Profile and add to the Order object passed to `SendOrderConfirmation` method.
Customer Profile	Create a new API for accessing customer communication preferences.
Order Shipping	Get communication preference and transport detail information from Customer Profile and add to the Order object passed to `SendShippingNotice` method.
Shopping Cart Management	Get communication preference and transport detail information from Customer Profile and add to the Order object passed to `SendAbandonedCartNotice` method.
Order Notifications	Change `SendOrderConfirmation`, `SendShippingNotice`, `SendAbandonedCartNotice` methods to be able to send emails, SMS, or both.
	Integrate a new third-party SMS API and add API configuration parameters to the configuration file.
	Change the `SendOrderConfirmation` logic to make sure we are still sending an order confirmation email to the shipping department even if the customer is getting an SMS message.
	Add new Message Formatter methods for all three notice types that now need to support SMS.

You wonder aloud whether this same effort will have to happen again if another notification preference comes along. It feels like the system, despite being relatively new, is not aging well as changes and new features are added. One of your teammates mentioned they felt the level of coupling in the system was high since such a small change had such a large ripple effect. Someone else wonders if we should redesign the whole notification system given the extent of changes that will be required and what we have learned that will allow us to "do it right" the next time. This is a hallmark of a team and design that is suffering under the weight of unnecessary complexity and entropy within their system. What started as a design that seemed to adapt to the changes became a burden, which progressively slowed the team down. If you have spent any time in this industry, you know what it is like to be on a team whose productivity curve starts to flatten over time, as shown in Figure 4-17.

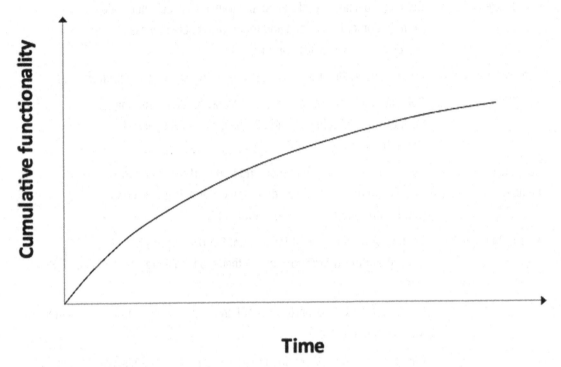

Figure 4-17. *Gradual decay in team productivity that can occur over time*

You decide to present two options back to the product owner: (1) changes to the existing system to support the new feature and (2) a redesign that will support the new feature and improve the overall design to minimize the impact of these types of features in the future. You are concerned that the amount of additional time to do the redesign, which will be rework, will not go over well given the constant pressure to add more new features. The product owner liked the talk of increased velocity and productivity with the redesign and endorsed that option.

The Redesign

You call a team meeting to gather input and insights from your team to help drive the redesign you are working on. There is good conversation and a consensus of what should be done. Given how obvious some of these conclusions are, you wonder why no one had thought of this when the project was started. The results of these discussions boiled down to three key conclusions:

- The Order Processing subsystem (and other subsystems) contains a significant amount of logic for sending order notices. If we encapsulate more of this logic in our Order Notification subsystem, we should be able to limit the impact of future notification changes to only our subsystem. This would include handling emails to suppliers in the same workflow as the order confirmation emails.

- Replacing the SMTP service with a third-party API meant changes to the Message Sender module and a lot of regression testing of the logic. We should isolate these types of changes to reduce the impact on regression testing.

- Sending email notices to the shipping department seems like a hack, and it feels like our system should not be involved. It would make more sense for the Order Processing subsystem to send the message themselves by accessing an API designed by the shipping department.

Based upon these conclusions, you decide on a new design that includes the following:

- Simplification of each of the notification methods to not include any messaging-specific data. Instead, your subsystem will interact with the Customer Profile subsystem to get notification preferences.

- Build an API access module for both SMTP and SMS that will abstract the details of the API interactions, and will also interact with the configuration file, to get any necessary parameters. The logic in the Message Sender is simplified as a result.

- Eliminate the special shipping department emails since the Order Processing subsystem will now take care of them.

- Rename your subsystem to "Notifications" to reflect the true responsibility of the subsystem.

During the design review with your team, someone points out that if the Message Sender is no longer talking directly to these APIs, we can start writing unit tests for this module by using dependency injection for the API access modules. This is another positive step in the right direction.

Figure 4-18 shows a sample workflow of the new Notification subsystem. Listing 4-5 shows the details of the redesigned APIs for the notification messages.

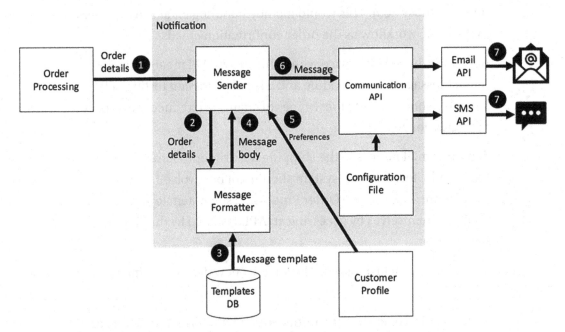

Figure 4-18. *Redesign of the notification subsystem*

Listing 4-5. Simplified notification interface

```
public interface IMessageSender
{
        void SendOrderNotice(OrderDetails details);
        void SendShippingNotice(ShippingDetails details);
        void SendAbandonedCartEmail(CartDetails details);
}
```

What Critical Thought Might Have Uncovered

When this project began, the team designed their subsystems and the details of their subsystems based upon the requirements known at the time. Stop and think about that statement (and the likelihood you have also done this). By designing against the current requirements, they were setting themselves up for trouble when new feature opportunities started presenting themselves. To be clear, the team did not make a conscious decision to *only* design against the current requirements. The problem is, they did not have a structured process for analyzing and decomposing the system to enable future change. Their system design resulted from a series of decisions that were made in the moment and with no criteria or constraints for helping them make their decisions. This is how an incredible amount of software is currently designed and developed today, which is why all of you who are reading this can relate to the story we just told.

Once their system had matured, the inevitable pain points started to become quite clear. The team began recognizing patterns and practices that they knew weren't right but could not put their finger on the cause until they sat down and decided to redesign the system with the benefit of their experiences. That redesign effort gave them space for some critical thinking, but unfortunately, it was done after the fact and will not prevent the significant rework required to improve the design.

Tactical vs. Strategic Development

The combination of a lack of software engineering literacy and the near-constant pressure to deliver new features and fixes pushes many development teams toward this more tactical approach to software development. By tactical, we mean that the actions and decisions being made by developers and development teams are driven primarily by the need to accomplish the specific task at hand. This could be the overall design for the system given what is known today or the task of making a specific change to satisfy a new feature requirement. These teams are making decisions based upon completing the current task so that they can move on to the next task.

When you are spending significant time and effort completing tasks, taking the time to consider the impact these design decisions might have on the future maintainability of the system rarely happens. Sometimes it is recognized that the solution being implemented represents technical debt. This is either rationalized as necessary and unavoidable, or the individual convinces themselves that they will be able to come back and "do it right" at a later time. As mentioned earlier, each of these decisions is unlikely to be significant on their own, but over time will lead to the inevitable "death by a thousand cuts."

The alternative to tactical software design and development is to be more strategic. When we are driven by a strategic mindset, we are constantly looking past the here and now and recognizing that our ultimate goal and responsibility is not to simply deliver the next feature but to continuously enable agility in our system. The ultimate goal being the ability to effectively respond to new opportunities over the entire lifetime of our system. Every decision must be weighed against this ultimate goal.

Strategic design and development starts with how we decide to decompose our system. In our earlier case study, the original design was based on satisfying the known, current requirements. If, on the other hand, the team had a process or method for system decomposition and design that focused on understanding current requirements and identifying likely areas of future change (and then encapsulating those areas), they would have avoided the whole mess. In fact, they might even come up with a design that is even better than the one they came up with during the redesign effort.

Systems tend to change in a handful of ways that can be discretely analyzed during the design process:

- Feature workflow logic

- Algorithms (e.g., pricing, tax calculations, etc.)

- External dependencies being used (e.g., cloud services, APIs, etc.)

- Data storage and structure

Personal experience and an understanding of the anticipated road maps for systems can provide insight that makes anticipating change something more than just a guess. This is not about trying to anticipate specific future features. It's about recognizing that any software system in use will be under constant maintenance to add new capabilities, improve existing capabilities, and/or take advantage of new technologies. Given our experience and insights, an initial analysis of the likely areas of change for notification systems might have identified the following:

- Methods of communication (e.g., Email, SMS, etc.)

- External dependencies (e.g., external SMTP and SMS services)

- Types of messages that need to be sent (i.e., not just order notices)

- Other parts of the platform that might need to be notified when things happen (e.g., shipping department)

As new feature requests come in, the team will be able to analyze the implementation of these new features against a coherent architecture, based upon minimizing the impact of change. They will determine how the new change fits into the architecture and if architectural changes need to be made to accommodate the new capability. An overall system design based upon sound principles becomes something that is constantly protected, nurtured, and maintained. It takes this level of active management of the design to avoid the entropy and decay that will otherwise creep into the system. When successful, it dramatically changes a team's trajectory and moves them toward consistent, sustainable agility and velocity.

Case Study Wrap-Up: Common Errors in Judgment

This case study aimed to provide a realistic scenario of what a common development experience is for many software development teams. It intentionally includes some of the most common errors in judgment that we see and have experienced. Again, errors in judgment are not intentional poor decisions but result from people making decisions without the knowledge or skill they need. One of this book's main goals is to help arm you with the knowledge to avoid or minimize these errors in judgment. Our experience has shown us that the reasons for most errors in judgment fall into a handful of categories:

- Lack of a design identity and a defined/disciplined methodology

- Decomposing systems based upon requirements instead of change

- Thinking tactically instead of strategically

- Lack of understanding of core principles and the impacts of design decision trade-offs

- Allowing material design decisions to be made by anyone

- Stagnant mental models for software systems

Lack of a Design Identity and a Defined/Disciplined Methodology

The team is not using a defined system, process, or method for taking a complex system and breaking it down into individual components at a class/service/module level. Many organizations have individuals who are responsible for defining the "big blocks" (e.g., the Order Notification subsystem), but when you look inside of these subsystems, it often looks like it was designed by different people with different "styles." These types of systems are very difficult to understand and maintain. Everyone who reads this book will know what we are talking about. Anytime you are asked to make a change in a part of the system designed and built by someone else, you end up spending enormous amounts of time trying to understand how that system works.

When there is a consistent design identity for a team, each piece of software looks like it was designed, not just by one person, but the *same* person. Ideally, when someone moves from the Notification subsystem to work in the Order Processing subsystem, they can look at the solution in this new system and understand what every module is doing and how things will work together.

Decomposing Systems Based upon Requirements Instead of Change

It seems to be quite natural for developers to decompose systems based upon the known requirements today. If you have ever been responsible for designing a system, I am confident you have made this error in judgment. The problem with decomposing against current requirements is that the decisions made during this process become more tactical (solving the current problem) instead of strategic (designing for continuous agility). As we mentioned before, the primary criteria for decomposing and designing software systems should be to enable change to occur more elegantly by encapsulating the areas of the system that are likely to change.

As we will see later on in this chapter, designing for change is done in other (i.e., non-software) systems. As both Juval Löwy[1] and software engineering pioneer David Parnas[2] point out, designing for change is less of a software-specific principle to be

---

[1]Löwy, Juval. 2020. *Righting Software*. Addison-Wesley Professional.

[2]Parnas, D.L. 1979. "Designing Software for Ease of Extension and Contraction." Proceedings of the Third International Conference on Software Engineering, May 1978, pp. 264–277.

followed and more of a systems engineering principle. The more we adopt principles shared with other types of systems, the more likely we are to design and build successful systems.

Thinking Tactically Instead of Strategically

Once a system is designed and the team is developing and maintaining the system, there will almost always be a perceived tension between doing things "right" and getting things done. In our case study, the "Order Notices for Shipping" feature should have been done in the Order Processing subsystem, but they had limited availability. Instead, another (less desirable) approach was taken. On its own, this decision would not result in the decay of the system. As we have discussed, these small decisions accumulate over time and lead to the system decay we must avoid. This decision was an example of thinking tactically – prioritizing the completion of the task at hand without regard for its long-term impact. We need to continuously balance tactical thinking with strategic thinking. This helps us avoid feeling like we are constantly asked to compromise good design practices and patterns.

Lack of Understanding of Core Concepts and Principles and the Impacts of Design Decision Trade-offs

The more we understand the core concepts and principles behind good design, the better armed we will be to argue for the more strategic solutions over the tactical ones. There are three core concepts and principles that must guide our software design decision-making: Coupling, Cohesion, and Information Hiding. Coupling (the strength of the relationship between two parts of a system (i.e., loose vs. tight) and cohesion (the degree to which elements inside a module relate or belong together) are familiar terms to most people in this career field. However, these two concepts are not understood at a deep enough level to enable sound, critical thought and evaluation of trade-offs on a day-to-day basis. The third one, information hiding, is a principle that has been around since the early 1970s, but most individuals in our field are unaware of the concept as well as the author of it, David Parnas. We will be discussing these core principles in detail later in this chapter.

Allowing Material Design Decisions to Be Made by Anyone

We routinely see individual developers making what we would consider to be architectural design decisions without much discussion or oversight. Examples would be deciding to create a new class or service, creating a new interface or data contract, and even redesigning whole parts of the system. Nothing will create more chaos than to have everyone working on the system making unilateral changes. This is particularly problematic in the absence of: a consistent design identity, a design that encapsulates changes, and a firm understanding of the core principles to be followed.

Regardless of the level of maturity of the individuals or the system, there must be an individual who maintains the overall "big picture" and actively protects the system design's integrity, and the adoption and application of sound software principles. You would be hard-pressed to find systems designed in other fields that do not have a chief engineer ensuring that the whole system is developed consistently with how it was designed. We will dive deeper into this chief engineer role in Chapter 7 and discuss their importance and responsibilities.

Stagnant Mental Models for Software Systems

The last 20 years have seen a significant shift in how scalable, reliable software systems are designed. Companies like Netflix, Salesforce.com, and Amazon have demonstrated how to build massively scalable software systems that handle user traffic beyond anything most of us will ever encounter in our careers. These systems are hosted on cloud platforms and are designed to provide 24/7 availability while constantly being revised and updated. To achieve these outcomes, the architects of these systems had to embrace and understand the core principles of software system design. They transitioned their mental model of software systems from monolithic, object-oriented systems to systems built on services that interact to provide the features and capabilities they require. They understand the challenges of managing data and state. This drove them to create more stateless or state-aware services, rather than bundling state and logic, as they might have been taught in school.

Unfortunately, most developers in our industry have not had a chance to work on systems like these. Their experience is more likely to be in maintaining client-server systems that were designed to be hosted on a single server. What's more, if they happened to have come from a formal computer science education in college, the only programming model they were exposed to was likely object-orientation. The notion of teaching a programming model that supports the design of service-based systems that can address the types of problems and applications being developed today, has not yet reached our education system. As a result, we have an enormous knowledge and skills gap in our talent pools. When these developers are assigned to design and build a modern service-based system, they naturally rely on their old mental models for how software should be designed and built. As the adage goes, when all you have is a hammer, everything looks like a nail.

Core Concepts and Principles of Modern System Design

As mentioned earlier, one of the main categories of errors in judgment is a lack of a firm understanding of core concepts and principles that must guide our software design decision-making: Coupling, Cohesion, and Information Hiding. In this section, we will briefly cover the more commonly known coupling and cohesion concepts and do a deep dive into the lesser-known principle of information hiding.

Coupling and Cohesion

Coupling in systems is the degree to which various parts of a system are interdependent. In general, the more interdependent they are, the tighter the coupling. There are a variety of ways in which modules within a simple system become coupled. The most straightforward is when one module calls an operation or method on another module. The two modules become interdependent, and the degree to which they are coupled is determined by the way the operation or method is designed. The coupling might be loose or tight or somewhere in between.

Cohesion is the sibling of coupling and refers to the degree to which functions and logic within a module are related to one another. High cohesion means the module contains highly related logic and functions. Low cohesion means the opposite. An example of a highly cohesive module is a sales tax module that does nothing but calculate sales tax. An example of a low cohesion module is an order totaling module where you might combine the calculation of product price, sales tax, and discounts in a single method or function.

Another way to think about cohesion is whether the business logic within the module is likely to change at the same time. For example, in our sale tax module, a change to the sales tax will affect all the business logic in the module. Within our order totaling module example, these same tax changes would only impact the logic related to tax calculations.

Key Point   As a rule of thumb, we should aim to design and maintain systems that are *loosely coupled* and *highly cohesive*. Doing so will result in more isolated changes as we extend and maintain the system. The opposite would be a tightly coupled, low cohesion system where every change we make has a ripple effect throughout the system (and makes our lives miserable).

The concepts of coupling and cohesion in software engineering are well known and documented even if not well understood by the rank-and-file developer. For this reason, we are not going to dive deep into these concepts within this book. However, as a developer, you must have a firm grasp of these concepts. It is important to recognize the degree of coupling and cohesion in the software you are working on and in the decisions you are making on a daily basis. The book *Code Complete*[3] by Steve McConnell is an excellent resource for deepening your understanding.

By themselves, simply understanding coupling and cohesion will not consistently get us to the outcomes we want with our software designs. They are properties of a system as opposed to a methodology for achieving minimal coupling and maximum cohesion. We briefly discuss them because of their important role as core concepts. You need to understand them to successfully and consistently design and develop scalable, maintainable systems. Something we will spend some more time with, because it is not as well understood and documented, is the principle of Information Hiding.

Information Hiding

In 1972, David Parnas wrote a seminal paper titled "On the Criteria To Be Used in Decomposing Systems into Modules."[4] While the paper itself is quite valuable, it is also interesting and informative to read how it came about (see "The secret history

---

[3]McConnell, Steven C. 2004. *Code Complete*, 2nd ed. Microsoft Press.

[4]Parnas, David L. 1972. "On the Criteria to Be Used in Decomposing Systems into Modules." *Communications of the ACM* 5, no. 12 (December): 1053–1058.

of information hiding"[5]). As an electrical engineer, Parnas was quite familiar with the process of designing complex non-software systems by assembling smaller components and modules, each with relatively simple and straightforward interfaces. It was a natural approach to handling complexity that had been proven in other fields of engineering. In 1969, he was involved in a software development project in which he recognized, but could not quite define, irregularities in software system designs that he knew were "ugly." This experience led him to research that revealed a core principle that should drive the decomposition of software systems to ensure their designs were "beautiful," which means they would be easy to understand, maintain, and extend with new features and capabilities. This principle became known as information hiding.

The key insight behind information hiding is that as information is distributed across a set of modules (e.g., services or objects), the modules sharing this information become coupled to some extent. If extending or modifying the system causes changes to the nature of this information, then all the modules will have to change. This is something we have all encountered and was demonstrated in our earlier case study. The information hiding principle states that information distribution and the impact of change should be minimized by (1) isolating aspects likely to change within modules and (2) creating interfaces between these modules that contain the bare minimum of information that is static and not impacted by change. The key outcome that expert system architects like Löwy[6] and Parnas[7] promote is to allow change and volatility within the modules in such a way that it does not impact other modules.

Like any skill, decomposing systems using information hiding is something that will take some focus and energy. Once you have developed some competency, you will begin to see systems differently, and it will become easier for you to work through the process.

In a nutshell, the process involves looking at the overall scope of the system to identify likely subsystems that will contain and encapsulate major portions of the system behavior. In an ecommerce system, the examples would be Processing Orders, Notifications, Shipping, etc. Each of these subsystems will provide discrete, fairly isolated capabilities that, in combination, will provide the desired capabilities and features of the system (e.g., buying a product online). Information hiding plays a role in evaluating

---

[5]Manfred Broy and Ernst Denert (Eds.). 2002. *Software Pioneers: Contributions to Software Engineering*. Springer-Verlag, Berlin, Heidelberg.

[6]Löwy, Juval. 2020. *Righting Software*. Addison-Wesley Professional.

[7]Parnas, D.L. 1979. "Designing Software for Ease of Extension and Contraction." Proceedings of the Third International Conference on Software Engineering, May 1978, pp. 264–277.

the choice of these subsystems even at this high level. Changes we make to how orders are processed or notifications are sent should not materially impact other areas of the system.

The process for designing for change continues down into these subsystems as we decompose the subsystem into modules, classes, services, etc. Now we begin to analyze and think through the various aspects of the subsystem to identify likely areas of change as we continue to grow and enhance the subsystem. Here we can also rely on some typical areas of business systems that will guide our analysis. Building upon the previous list of areas in a system that are likely to change, these are things that typically change over the lifetime of a software product:

- The way we store and access data

    - Data structure

    - Storage platforms

- Algorithms and business rules

    - Examples include price and discount calculations, business decision formulas

- External service and hardware dependencies

    - It is always good practice to isolate your system from any third-party dependencies, both for reliability and the flexibility to replace these dependencies with another option

- APIs used by external UI clients

    - These might contain operations used by external clients (UI, third parties) to access the specific sequences and operations that orchestrate features in our system

- Integrations to unstable or legacy code

    - Like third-party dependencies, parts of your system that are under constant maintenance due to instability should be heavily isolated from creating changes in other parts of the system.

Let's use our case study as an example of where the principle of information hiding is violated and what a better design that adheres to this principle could look like. Recall that the Order Processing subsystem and the Notification subsystem interact to send customer order notices when an order is placed. Also, recall that the way this was originally implemented, the Order Processing subsystem gathered and provided the necessary information to the Notification subsystem to send these customer notices. With this design, when changes occurred to customer order notification requirements, the Order Processing subsystem was usually required to make some of the changes in their subsystem to support this. This is a symptom of excessive information distribution and a violation of the information hiding principle.

So, how do we apply this principle in this case? First, we need to ask ourselves where the business logic should reside in order to send customer order notifications. By now, we should all agree that this should reside in the Notification subsystem. Next, a little critical thinking about likely areas of change would lead us to assume that order notifications are likely to change over time. Given this, our design should reflect our desire to encapsulate this change within the order notifications subsystem and create an interface to this subsystem that provides the bare minimum of information to initiate the sending of these notifications. This type of design will likely survive and remain unchanged regardless of changes that might occur within the subsystem as new notification requirements emerge. A first stab at this might be to add a method to the interface called SendOrderNotice along with the other notice methods that each take a single parameter of an Order Id instead of the complex order object that was in the original design, as shown in Listing 4-6.

Listing 4-6. Notification subsystem API with simplified parameter

```
public interface IMessageSender
{
        void SendOrderNotice(int orderId);
        void SendShippingNotice(int orderId);
        void SendAbandonedCartEmail(int orderId);
}
```

Now, let's go back to the Order Processing subsystem and ask ourselves, "What knowledge does this subsystem *really* need for notifications to be sent?" Does Order Processing need to know that notices are sent at all? Can we simplify this interface even more? It is extremely important that we continually ask ourselves, "What is the absolute minimum amount of information I need to exchange?"

The Order Processing subsystem is where orders are created, so naturally, these types of events in this subsystem would initiate a variety of other workflows. Let's think more deeply about what the Order Processing subsystem needs to do. We can conclude that the *only* thing the subsystem needs to know about Notification is that it needs to provide notice of order events like order placed or order failed. The simplified interface to the Notification subsystem could be made even simpler to hide even more details behind the interface, as shown in Listing 4-7.

Listing 4-7. Notification subsystem API with a single method

```
public interface IMessageSender
{
        void OrderEvent(int eventId, int eventType);
}
```

It should be clear now that we have greatly reduced the amount of information about order notifications that the Order Processing subsystem will be aware of. This also means we have significantly reduced the coupling between these two subsystems and dramatically reduced the possibility that future changes to order notifications will impact the Order Processing subsystem. Overall maintainability and agility of the system have been improved.

Key Point   As a rule of thumb, when designing an interface, always start by asking yourself what is the *absolute minimum* amount of data and information that can be passed between modules/component. This should be the default initial proposal for the design of the interface.

We could take this a step further by asking ourselves whether the Order Processing subsystem needs to know about the existence of the Notification subsystem. As it is currently designed, the Order Processing subsystem will have a dependency on the IMessageSender interface, which is implemented by the Notifications subsystem. We can take advantage of a common tool in modern application development and insert a message bus or queueing component between the Order Processing subsystem and the Notification subsystem. This would mean that the Order Processing subsystem would now just publish an order event message to a generic event queue that is being watched by the Notification subsystem (and possibly other subsystems). When the Notification subsystem sees an event message on the queue, it takes the message and proceeds with its notification logic just as if it would have when the OrderEvent method of its interface was called. Figure 4-19 shows a diagram of how this would work. Queues and message busses are powerful tools to further decouple parts of a system. They are generally used for interactions between subsystems like our Order Processing and Notification example.

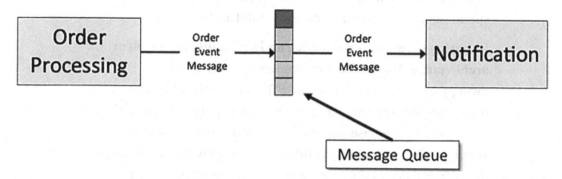

Figure 4-19. *Using a queue to decouple Order Processing and Notification subsystems*

Fully understanding the purpose and goals of information hiding is critical to making the best decisions about how software systems are decomposed and what leads to excessive coupling between components. Every decision we make related to interactions between components has consequences. We must better equip ourselves to reveal these consequences and have a firm, articulate reason for the choices we make if we want to reduce errors in judgment. The information hiding principle should be the primary tool in our toolbox.

Trade-offs Are the Norm

Now, you may argue that not sending the information needed to the Notification subsystem means that additional database calls need to be executed to get this information, even though the Order Processing subsystem already had it. While this is true, it does not mean we are making a bad decision. This is a classic example of making a trade-off, choosing or compromising between two desirable but incompatible choices. Very few decisions we make in software development, and engineering in general, are obvious, black and white, no-brainers. Most decisions involve trading off one thing for something else. Some examples of these types of trade-offs are as follows:

Using an off-the-shelf component with limited customization vs. writing one from scratch. In the former, you get something that may not have all of the bells and whistles but is already written, used, and supported, which means there is less risk of additional effort down the road. In the latter, you have an option that you will be able to bend to your will, but you will have to spend significant time and energy to build and support.

Choosing between performance and scalability for a system architecture. Many system components, like databases, must process transactions serially. This means they become a bottleneck for performance as more transactions run through the system. In this case, the choice might be made to design the system so that operations are queued to keep the user experience more responsive, at the expense of having certain operations complete in real-time. An example might be a user changing a profile setting that is not immediately reflected in the application.

In our case, it is more beneficial to the overall system to reduce the coupling between these two subsystems at the expense of an additional, discrete database query. We would make this trade-off almost without exception. The long-term impact on maintainability and agility provided by minimized coupling far outweighs the small impact of the additional database queries.

Information Hiding Hierarchies

When information hiding becomes the driving principle for how systems are decomposed and designed, we will find that the principle will be applied to various hierarchies within the system. At the highest level, it should be used to determine how the system is decomposed into subsystems (by isolating collections of related business logic like order processing, order notifications, etc.). Within the subsystems, we must also ensure that the subsystem components are also properly applying this principle by continuing the decomposition based upon encapsulating likely areas of change and simplifying the interfaces between these components.

When done correctly, a completely new module that implements the same interface as the current module, but has entirely different internal behavior, could replace the current module with no changes to the rest of the system. An example from our use case is the way the email systems were used to send notifications. Had the Notification subsystem team understood and applied information hiding to the decomposition of their subsystem, they would have realized that a lot of information related to interaction with the SMTP service was spread throughout the subsystem. A better design based upon information hiding might have led to the Communication API module much sooner, as shown in Figure 4-20 and Listing 4-8.

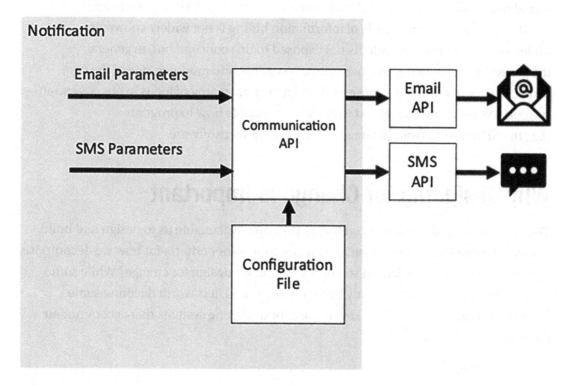

Figure 4-20. *Hiding message delivery details in the communication API module*

Listing 4-8. Example communication module interface

```
public interface ICommunicationApi
{
        void SendEmail(string emailAddress, string subject,
                        string body);
        void SendSms(string mobileNumber, string body);
}
```

The rest of the subsystem that uses this interface would have knowledge of the required components of an email (Email Address, Subject, Body) but would not know the details of creating and sending an email. When the decision was made to swap out the SMTP service for a third-party email service, the Communication API module could have been replaced with a new version that implements the same interface but encapsulates the logic to interact with the third party instead. The rest of the subsystem would not know this change had occurred, nor would it need that knowledge.

Unfortunately, the principle of information hiding is not widely known or understood. Not only are students not exposed to this concept, but, in general, the proper methods to decompose software systems into modules, one of the core competencies necessary for successful design, is not an area of focus in our education systems. We are more concerned with teaching people how to program (i.e., manufacture software) instead of how to engineer software.

Why Designing for Change Is Important

The application of the information hiding principle will enable us to design and build systems designed for change instead of using some other criteria for how we decompose and design systems. So why is it so important that we design for change? While some of the answers to this have already been demonstrated, it is worth devoting some discussion to it. There are three key reasons for designing systems that accommodate change:

- Design stamina

- Increased comprehensibility

- Meeting the demands of modern applications and business agility

Design Stamina

Martin Fowler wrote an essay a few years back titled "The Design Stamina Hypothesis."[8] In this essay, Fowler discusses the trade-off of no design vs. "good" design. He argues that velocity may initially be higher for the "no design" team, but eventually (and

---

[8]https://martinfowler.com/bliki/DesignStaminaHypothesis.html

quite quickly) the "good design" team will surpass them, not by increasing their own velocity, but by the dramatic decrease in the velocity of the "no design" team as shown in Figure 4-21.

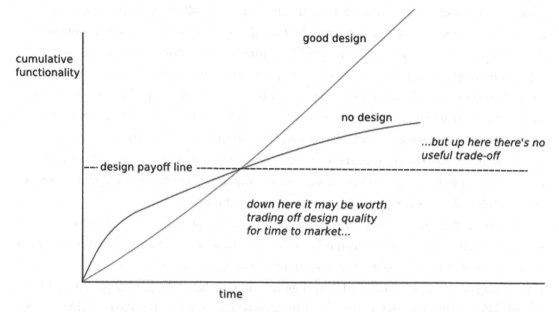

Figure 4-21. *The Design Stamina Hypothesis (Source: Martin Fowler* `https://` `martinfowler.com/bliki/DesignStaminaHypothesis.html`)

I have personally drawn this diagram on countless whiteboards over the years. In every case, we see head nods acknowledging the velocity trend of the "no design" team. Anyone who has spent any time in this career field will have experienced this. Our previous case study covered this experience. Fowler does not define "good" design specifically but does argue that some upfront investment in good design will pay off over time. This has been our experience as well, and this crossover point where the design effort starts paying off can happen within weeks of the start of a project.

A key attribute of a good design that achieves this desired trajectory is that the design does not resist change but rather accommodates it. This is why designing for change and effectively applying information hiding is essential. As discussed earlier in this chapter, if we simply design against the current known requirements, we are optimizing for today without considering how future changes might impact our design decisions and the trade-offs that we made. This is a classic example of our errors in judgment.

Increased Comprehensibility

Software that effectively applies information hiding is easier for developers to understand and comprehend, which reduces their cognitive load and makes them more effective and productive. The reason for this is simple. We often hear the old axiom that a developer spends ten times as much effort reading code than writing code. Before implementing a new feature, we are spending time reading code to understand how something works and the impact of the change on the entire system. We do not want to inadvertently introduce some side effects or unintended behavior. We have to spend so much time reading code because systems are often constructed in violation of the information hiding principle, which means information is unnecessarily spread out across many modules rather than encapsulated behind simple interfaces. The resulting excessive coupling means our systems are more fragile and brittle. Any change we make in a module will likely require changes elsewhere in the system.

We think about increasing comprehensibility and reducing developer cognitive load in terms of the required "field of view." The field of view for a developer making a change is the scope of the system that they need to review and understand, in order to determine what changes are to be made, and how they should be testing those changes to ensure no side effects. When we have high coupling in a system, we say that the developer's field of view is large.

Figure 4-22 illustrates a system where a developer needs to make a change to an application that might involve changing the structure of a database table. Unfortunately, the specific details of the database structure are known and relied upon by several modules in the system. As a result, many modules will need to be updated to accommodate this change (boxes with bold outlines).

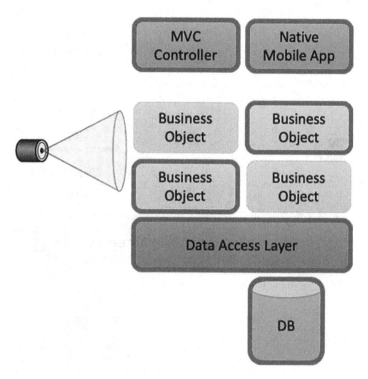

Figure 4-22. *Wide developer field-of-view*

Alternatively, suppose the system had been designed in such a way that the database structure, something that should not be exposed system-wide, is isolated primarily to the data access layer. In that case, the areas to be changed are reduced substantially. The developer now has what we would call a narrow field-of-view, as shown in Figure 4-23.

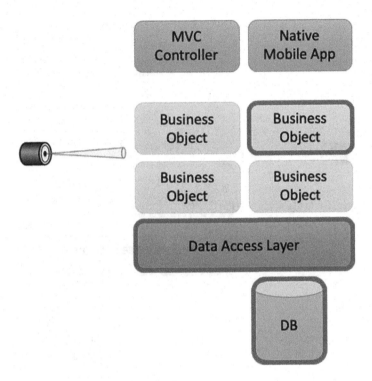

Figure 4-23. *Narrow developer field-of-view*

Consistently minimizing the developer field-of-view (and the resulting reduction in cognitive load) can only be accomplished if the system is designed so that future changes impact a minimal number of modules.

Meeting the Demands of Modern Applications and Business Agility

The final reason to embrace designing systems based upon encapsulating change is because, quite frankly, the modern cloud-based, distributed systems we need to build to tackle today's problems demand it. If we try to use our old object-oriented, monolithic, client-server programming models on today's problems, we will be met with consistent failure. For the last 50 years, we have slowly been on a trajectory and path to solving problems that require the scale and agility that loosely coupled, highly cohesive, service-based systems provide. The examples around us are plentiful. What once might have been a successful desktop application for managing your contacts and business leads in the 1990s has now become a massive cloud-based application platform for business and sales automation. Our product update rhythm of annual or quarterly releases has become weekly, and sometimes daily, pushing of new features and bug fixes to production.

One might assume that the rapid pace of innovation and demand for developing new ideas and products in the modern world would require processes and methods that take shortcuts on planning and critical thought in order to be responsive to the business and market. The exact opposite is true. Since 2000 we have been involved in numerous software startup and innovation efforts. The rapid innovation and response required for these efforts accelerates when customers start using and engaging with the product. This is when our agility is tested. It is in these periods of rapid change and feature enhancements when designing for change really shines and provides us the responsiveness we need.

There have been several times when entrepreneurs have approached us to ask us to build something, and they want us to just start coding. Their reasoning goes something like this: "Let's just hack something together now to get it out in people's hands. If it gets traction, we will rebuild it correctly." The sad reality is the only scenario that will give them the time to completely rebuild their application is when no one is using it. Once a product starts to get traction, the overarching priority will be to respond to the inevitable customer inputs and feature requests. Agility is one of the keys to success and designing for change is what enables this agility.

Managing Complexity in Other Systems

In the 1970s, David Parnas wondered why software systems were not designed similarly to how other non-software systems were designed. This was the genesis of his paper on information hiding. Over the last 20 years, we have seen several companies and individuals lead the charge to push our industry in a direction that mirrors the way other systems are designed. Companies like Netflix and Amazon, and individuals like Juval Löwy from IDesign,[9] have been champions of services-based approaches to building scalable, distributed systems that move us toward more loosely coupled solutions. Their efforts are bringing us closer in line with how complexity is managed in other systems. Even principles we have come to know in software development, like encapsulation,

---

[9]`www.idesign.net`

design for change, abstraction, modularity, behavior through interaction, and separation of concerns are found in the set of principles in the systems engineering body of knowledge.[10]

Thinking back to my own experience as a systems engineer at McDonnell Douglas, it is clear that the architects of the avionics subsystems on those aircraft understood how to apply these principles of systems engineering that also apply to pure software systems. After some time to familiarize myself, I was able to easily name and describe all of the subsystems in the avionics system and how they interacted to perform the various functions of the aircraft. I was not overwhelmed by the need to understand every detail of the whole system to do my job. Changes that we made to these systems tended to be localized through proper encapsulation. These systems were designed with a firm understanding that humans are only capable of managing about five to nine concepts simultaneously.[11]

The point of paying attention to the principles behind how other systems are designed is to recognize that principles like information hiding, and concepts like the level of coupling and cohesion are not specific to software systems, but apply to systems in general. The more we start to treat software systems like other systems (instead of systems with their own first principles[12]), the better we will be at creating mental models of what well-designed and decomposed software systems should be.

Choosing a Design Methodology

In this chapter, we have discussed the importance of system decomposition and design. We have devoted considerable space to help you understand the elements of good design and decomposition. None of this will help you be successful unless you can pair this knowledge with a single methodology that you can reliably and consistently use to

---

[10]SEBoK Editorial Board. 2020. *The Guide to the Systems Engineering Body of Knowledge* (SEBoK), v. 2.3, R.J. Cloutier (Editor in Chief). Hoboken, NJ: The Trustees of the Stevens Institute of Technology. Accessed April 6, 2021. www.sebokwiki.org. BKCASE is managed and maintained by the Stevens Institute of Technology Systems Engineering Research Center, the International Council on Systems Engineering, and the Institute of Electrical and Electronics Engineers Systems Council.

[11]Miller, G. 1956. "The magical number seven, plus or minus two: some limits on our capacity for processing information." *The Psychological Review.* 63: 81–97.

[12]A first principle is the basic building block or assumption that drives the development of processes and methods.

design and build modern applications and achieve the desired outcome of sustainable agility. While details of a specific methodology are out of the scope for this book, we have some recommendations and guidance to help you choose a process.

First, be wary of books, languages, or frameworks promoting simple approaches to system design that anyone can pick up in a weekend. The idea of a silver bullet to solve the design of complex systems is likely a trap. Getting this right and avoiding errors in judgment requires focus, skill, and effort. You can build bad designs in any framework or programming language that is out there.

Second, you will find that many books on software architecture lack detail on how to put their guidance into practice. We know; we've reviewed many of them over the years. These books tend to be very light in terms of criteria and considerations for taking a system and decomposing it into subsystems, subsystems into modules/ services, and so on.

Third, most programming models and system design techniques like Object-Oriented Analysis and Design do not properly make designing for change the key criteria for decomposing systems. Unless we make information hiding (and therefore designing for change) *the* key principle for designing systems, we will fail to achieve design stamina and sustainable agility.

We are aware of two methodologies that can be adopted to fill the role of your design methodology. The first is a process called "The Method," which was developed by Juval Löwy of IDesign, and is discussed and demonstrated in great detail in his book *Righting Software*.[13] We have extensive experience with this methodology and have used it on hundreds of projects. I am confident that choosing this approach will get you the results you desire, and this methodology would be our primary recommendation.

Another methodology that has gained some notoriety over the last few years is Domain-Driven Design, first developed by Eric Evans.[14] We are not as familiar with this technique. Still, it appears to meet the criteria of providing prescriptive guidance like "The Method," and indications are it could be implemented in such a way that design for change is a guiding principle.

---

[13]Löwy, Juval. 2020. *Righting Software*. Addison-Wesley Professional.

[14]Evans, Eric. 2003. *Domain-Driven Design: Tackling Complexity in the Heart of Software.* Addison-Wesley Professional.

Summary

If you have worked in this industry a while, no doubt you have had to work on a software system that has fallen victim to software rot and entropy. This reality should come as no surprise, given the lack of emphasis on system decomposition and design in our formal educational curriculum. Given the nature of the systems we are building today and the need for those systems to adapt as new opportunities present themselves, we cannot afford to design systems that need to be rebuilt every few years because they have become unmaintainable.

The key to designing and building sustainable software systems is to understand the foundational concepts and principles that enable sustainability. We must adopt a design and decomposition methodology that embraces these principles and makes design for change and application of the information hiding principle *the* key objective – something that we can see in other types of systems.

Finally, system design is not something that is done and then published. Software entropy can occur in any system, even in a well-designed system. Design must be continuously nurtured and protected by hands-on technical leaders. This type of technical leadership is critical, which is why we devoted Chapter 7 to this topic.

Key Takeaways

- **Many systems start out coherent**, but they decay as they attempt to accommodate change.

- **Errors in judgment are the root cause of design decisions that lead to software entropy**. These errors fall into a handful of categories:

  - Lack of a design identity and defined/disciplined methodology

  - Decomposing systems based upon requirements instead of change

  - Thinking tactically instead of strategically

  - Lack of understanding of core principles and the impacts of trade-offs we are making when we make design decisions

  - Allowing material design decisions to be made by anyone

- Stagnant mental models for software systems

- **Developers and architects must balance the tactical needs of development with the need to consider the strategic impacts of their decisions.**

- **It is essential that software developers understand, comprehend, and apply the principle of information hiding**, which enables us to design and build loosely coupled, highly cohesive systems that are designed for change.

- **The level of coupling and cohesion in a system are critical properties to recognize and actively manage**, as they directly impact the long-term agility and maintainability of the system and the developer's field of view and cognitive load when making changes.

- **Design for change is important** because (1) it enables our designs to be viable and agile much longer, (2) it makes them more comprehensible, and (3) modern applications and business agility demand it.

- **We can learn a lot about building modern scalable and maintainable software systems by studying how other complex systems are designed.**

- **Adopting an established, proven system design and decomposition based upon designing for change is essential.** Unfortunately, all methods – except for a few – stop short of providing the tools and prescriptions to take our decompositions down to a modules/service/class/interface level, which is necessary to be successful.

Now that we have a good understanding of what is required to design systems that age well, we can turn our attention to how we can ensure our developers are making good decisions as they build and maintain these systems.

CHAPTER 5

Developers "Falling into the Pit of Success"

Introduction

Success must be engineered, and failure must require falling outside of norms. We must engineer development practices and processes to ensure developers are successful. Leaving anything to chance will result in developers falling into the pit of failure. In this chapter, we will focus on those practices and processes that enable developers to consistently fall into the pit of success.

Reality Check

In Alfred Hitchcock's 1958 film Vertigo, the main character John falls in love with Madeleine when he falls into the water to save her. The literal falling in love is a common trope used in romantic comedies, but it also appears in this serious film.

Software development is ripe with opportunities to fail. Given how many chances we have to get it wrong, it is a wonder we ever get it right. Software development has little tolerance for error. A single misplaced character can stop an entire order from successful completion on an ecommerce system.

Much like John, the character from Vertigo, it is very easy to fall into a trap when making software, and it's much easier than falling into success. As developers, we are constantly "running with scissors," but then are surprised when we get hurt! We feel that we must move quickly to achieve the goals, yet we know that running in a room with our teammates carrying sharp things is a bad idea.

© Doug Durham and Chad Michel 2021
D. Durham and C. Michel, *Lean Software Systems Engineering for Developers*,
https://doi.org/10.1007/978-1-4842-6933-6_5

When we hire a new employee, we are basically handing them scissors and the command of "run quickly." What do we expect will happen? If we are set up for failure, we will more than likely fail.

Instead of setting developers up for failure, what about setting them up for success? If you asked developers what is the most likely cause of their failures, what do you think they would say? Here are some common failures I have heard:

- If only...

  - ... I had better requirements

  - ... The mockups were done before I started

  - ... The UI designs matched what we could do with the controls

  - ... It wasn't so difficult to test

  - ... I didn't get interrupted so much

  - ... I didn't run into difficult coding problems during an iteration

  - ... I had more time and didn't have to rush so much

This list of reasons for failure is common and consistent across many organizations and has not changed much over the years. We have done many things to reduce the impact of this list, but it is pretty much the same list.

A common tool that attempts to help is agile practices and processes. With agile processes, there are a few areas of focus that can significantly help with these problems. The first is shorter sprints or shorter time windows. These smaller windows limit some of the damage done by people going off into the weeds. These smaller sprints also help focus teams on what they are going to do now, which can help focus requirement gathering efforts to a limited set of the overall functionality. Better, more complete requirements are a huge improvement for developers. Another helpful focus of most agile processes is daily standup meetings. These standups keep everyone informed and focused on the task at hand.

While agile processes do help, they don't address many of the core issues that developers face. Developers can still fall into the pit of failure during agile projects. If you work at an agile development shop, do your developers continue to fail to get their work done in the iterations? If so, why? Their reasons may be in the list presented previously.

What does success look like? From a pure development point of view, success has several qualities. First, software projects should be successful most of the time.

Sprints (or iterations) should be successful almost all of the time. Do you feel like you successfully end sprints most of the time? How often does everyone get their stories done in the sprint? Second, software development should feel engineered, running like a finely tuned machine. It should not feel like a runaway train. Finally, are the developers enjoying the work? Software development should be fun and enjoyable. Software development is one-part problem solving, one-part creation, and one-part team sport. That should be fun.

A Developer's Life

It is easy to imagine what failure looks like since we have all experienced it. But let's go through a hypothetical developer's life on an agile team to illustrate a typical experience. This story will focus on a single developer who is still new to the team. We will call him Aaron.

Aaron's team consistently follows agile ceremonies, with standups, iteration planning, iteration pre-planning, and retrospectives. Each developer works autonomously on the team, and they don't have much time to mentor Aaron, as each developer is overbooked with work. Their sprints are one week in length. They start on Monday and end on Friday.

A Bad Week

Aaron showed up for work on Monday not knowing what he will work on this week, which is often stressful for many developers. He pulled down the latest code and merged it in with his code. But when he tries to run the solution on his machine, nothing works. He tries to flag down the other developers, but they are fighting through a few last-minute demo issues on their machines. Eventually, Aaron discovers that the other developers upgraded a UI framework they use. Unfortunately, he gets this information right before the meeting.

The team has its 9:00 a.m. iteration planning meeting. This meeting is scheduled for two hours, but often only lasts for one hour. Today's meeting will probably be shorter because the product owner won't be able to attend. The meeting starts with demos of the previous week's work. Each developer demos their work running on their own machines. The demos for the other developers go fine, each takes a little while to get set up to present, but they ultimately demo what they worked on.

Aaron's demo doesn't go so well. He did get the framework updated, but now he is getting some hard-to-diagnose errors while running the solution. He throws up his hands and admits that he doesn't know why it isn't working. The project manager gives him a disappointed look.

The meeting continues with the selection of stories and their assignment to developers. The other developers continue to work on some integrations with different third parties. They assign Aaron a single story: add a grid that lists all emails sent to a given customer in their CRM platform.

He gets his environment up and running again after the planning meeting but has to stop at 11:30 for team standup.

At this company, they have a whole company lunch on Mondays. During this meeting, an executive will usually present something about how the company is doing. Today's meeting is led by the CTO and he discusses the importance of getting things done. No exceptions should be made for not getting our commitments done. Aaron feels the glare of his PM for not getting things done in the last iteration.

After the long lunch, Aaron gets back to work on his new story. He is tasked with building a user interface that shows all emails sent to a particular client. During iteration planning, they brought up the desire to use their UI framework's data grid for this feature. After lunch, Aaron takes a couple of minutes to look at the data grid documentation. The data grid was recently updated by the manufacturer to the latest release. The update includes things like filtering, sorting, and pagination. All are features the client will probably want. After a quick look through the documentation, he looks at the emails table in the developer database. The table is sparse on information, and it contains "from," "to," "subject," "body," and "end date."

Aaron rolls up his sleeves and begins writing this new email grid. He starts by writing code to query the emails from the database. By the time the 3:00 p.m. code review meeting comes around, he is feeling good about his progress.

Since they don't have any code to look at in their 3:00 p.m. meeting, Aaron shows the other developers how the story is coming along. He shows them the new method he has added to their data repository. Everyone is encouraged by the progress, but they wonder if they should continue to build upon an older database framework that they use. Instead, they feel like upgrading to the latest and greatest version might help them, too. He starts updating the database framework.

At 4:00 p.m., the product owner decides to call a quick meeting so she can see product demos. About the time she calls the meeting, Aaron is neck-deep in migrating to the new database framework. So again, Aaron's demo fails.

During the first hour the following day, one of the other developers helps Aaron sort through the database framework issue. Aaron spends the rest of the morning rewriting his call in the new framework. At standup, Aaron arrives triumphantly. He can now retrieve the data from the database. He just needs to wire up the data grid and is feeling pretty good. He even dares to mention in standup, "I think I'll get done today."

He powered through and was able to stand up a grid in the UI. Wiring the grid up wasn't as easy as expected. It required some rework of his data access, but ultimately it came together pretty well.

Wednesday morning was great for Aaron. He walked through the UI a few times and made sure it looked good on a variety of browsers. A co-worker walked by and asked how he was doing. "Almost done," Aaron responded.

Standup couldn't come fast enough for Aaron. And once it started, he couldn't wait for his turn. Aaron demoed his grid to the group, expecting applause as a response, but received a quick rebuke from the UI designer. The UI designer pointed out that the grid would need pagination because there would be too much data on the page to show all of it at once. Aaron was less than excited by the miss on his part, but he did get some very encouraging feedback about the filtering and sorting capabilities. The product owner was in the standup and gave Aaron a thumbs up, even though it didn't have the pagination it needed.

Wednesday afternoon was kind of a reset for Aaron. Switching to pagination was a major change to his backend code. They did get lucky. Pagination was finally supported in their data grid because of the upgrade done the week before. But with enough focus time, Aaron thinks he could have the grid up and running again. Unfortunately, he has a weekly cross-team developer standup that typically lasts two hours, basically eating up most of his Wednesday afternoon.

Thursday morning arrives with Aaron feeling a little worried about what could go wrong next. He quickly gets to work on the grid changes. By the time standup arrives, he has everything working again.

During standup, he again demos his progress. This time to the resounding accolades of his teammates, and most importantly, the product owner. The product owner loves the grid, especially the filtering and sorting. Aaron finally has some success. He tells everyone he should be done within a few hours. He is now "really close."

Key Point   Don't be fooled. All of the following phrases are equivalent to meaning "not done" and should prompt concern: "I'm making good progress," "I just need a little bit more time," "I'm almost there," "I'm really close."

During lunch, Aaron and the rest of the team get an email that everything in QA is broken. Aaron doubts it is *everything*, but the team quickly regroups after lunch to take a look. Some stray logs imply it is potentially some communication issue with the backend, but no one is certain what has changed. The team quickly determines it is the database framework upgrade that Aaron did on Monday. After a very disappointing look from the project manager, Aaron drops what he is working on and dives into determining how his upgrade broke everything.

Aaron knows that this could be a disaster, so he works nervously and quickly. He tries different ways to reproduce the issue, but he can't. After a while, he notices that all the broken parts of the system use a particular UI control. He doesn't have time to dig into why because they have an iteration pre-planning meeting on Thursday afternoon that sucks up half of his Thursday work time.

Friday morning arrives with a broken QA and unfinished grid work (but close). Aaron is now officially stressed out. He can't figure out what is going on with that control. He is just ready to submit an issue to the publisher of the UI framework when he comes across a forum post about the UI control and learns there is an issue when it is hosted in a non-development setup. The control will be fixed in the next version of the UI framework, which should ship in two months. Aaron needs to have his work done by Monday and can't wait two months.

Aaron talks it over with the team, and they decide that the UI framework needs to be reverted. Aaron reverts the UI framework to the old version. This causes all sorts of churn in the grid, including the loss of some features like sorting and filtering. Aaron went from almost done to spending most of Friday night rewiring up the grid.

Monday morning arrives, and Aaron has completed his work for the sprint. He has a working grid. During their iteration planning, he shows the new grid to the team. Aaron feels triumphant until the product owner asks, "what happened to the sorting and filtering?"

Sound Familiar?

This story of a bad week for a developer might be fiction, but did each element feel like something you have heard before? Developers changing technologies without telling their peers. Developers upgrading technologies on a whim. People not understanding why developers missed a deadline. Requirements getting clarified after something is already implemented.

In this example, Aaron's job doesn't sound like a lot of fun, does it? Every day is a new disaster. He is most certainly not falling into the pit of success.

First off, randomly updating a framework is often not going to end well. This was an error in judgment. This type of decision needs to be communicated clearly. The team shouldn't have been praising the upgrade. Instead, they should have asked the hard question of why the framework was changed when the effort to implement and validate wasn't included in the sprint plan.

Second, starting the grid work without mockups or design from the UI designer was a big mistake. It all but guaranteed the need for rework. Not having a design before development starts will almost always end up in some form of rework, which is expensive and frustrating.

Third, the project manager blamed Aaron for not getting his work done, but he didn't factor in the UI framework change that broke Aaron's work. This change caused Aaron's work to not be demo-able on his machine. But the bigger problem here is that they were demoing from developer machines when they needed to be demoing from a QA environment where everyone's code was running in the same environment.

Fourth, Aaron's calendar feels pretty chopped up. He had a lot of regular meetings and some unexpected meetings. Figure 5-1 shows a snapshot of Aaron's calendar. Every day has a standup and a review time. It feels like he doesn't have a lot of time to do "deep work," something we will discuss later in this chapter.

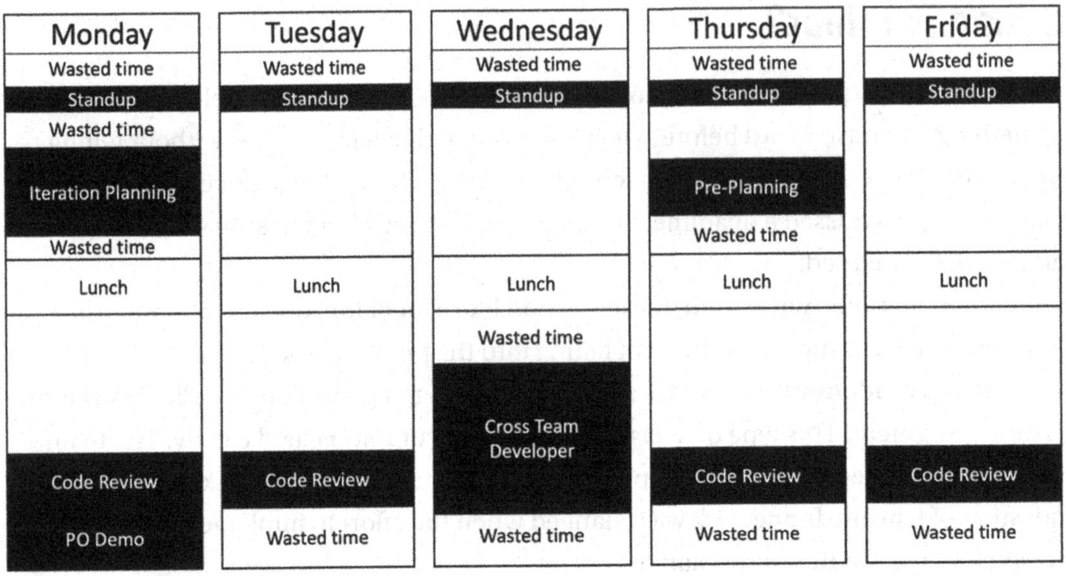

Monday	Tuesday	Wednesday	Thursday	Friday
Wasted time	Wasted time	Wasted time	Wasted time	Wasted time
Standup	Standup	Standup	Standup	Standup
Wasted time				
Iteration Planning			Pre-Planning	
Wasted time			Wasted time	
Lunch	Lunch	Lunch	Lunch	Lunch
		Wasted time		
		Cross Team Developer		
Code Review	Code Review		Code Review	Code Review
PO Demo	Wasted time	Wasted time	Wasted time	Wasted time

Figure 5-1. *An inefficient developer calendar*

This was not a great week for Aaron. Not only was he under constant scrutiny from the product manager, but he had to deal with changing requirements and changing technology. That is a lot of change to deal with in a single iteration, so it is amazing he achieved anything. He implemented the grid three times during the week, dealt with three framework changes, and had a project manager breathing down his neck the whole way. No developer wants to work like that!

Creating a Pit of Success for Developers

We want and need developers to be consistently successful, and every developer needs to be successful for a team to be successful. Successful software teams are more like football teams than basketball teams. With a basketball team, one excellent player can carry the team, like Michael Jordan in his prime. But in football, even really good players require really good players around them to be successful. In software, everyone has a role. If one developer is not meeting expectations, the entire team is impacted.

Consistent successful outcomes will only come as a result of a systematic and disciplined development process. The more systematic and disciplined we are, the more predictable our outcomes will be. This starts with following the same processes, over and over. Every new project needs to adhere to the same process. Sure, some projects might take longer and require more time on certain parts, but ideally, they should feel consistent.

What processes enable consistent success? Almost anything that puts critical thought upfront is good. Ideally, you want everyone to be thinking before doing. A good process should enable good critical thought and discourage rushing to put fingers to keyboards.

You can go too far. There must be a balance. You could create heavy, bureaucratic processes that do include critical thought, but forward progress would grind to a halt. Everything we do should enable us to move faster, not slower. If we add process steps that ultimately cause us to move slower, we should remove them. The key is to take a lean, lightweight approach to add processes and then build on to them as you see opportunities to fill gaps that represent leaving an outcome to chance or increased errors in judgment. Our goal should be to deliver the project on time and on budget while meeting the needs and quality expectations of the stakeholders.

The idea of moving faster by adding processes might strike some as surprising. We don't mean moving faster in the short term; we mean moving faster over the lifetime of a software product. We must set ourselves up to live with the software for years, not weeks. Recall from Chapter 2 that rework can destroy projects. Sometimes rework is disguised as integration at the end of a project or redesigns in the next version. This extra time can kill projects. To move faster, we must focus on quality.

The question you are probably asking now is where to start. Our recommendation is to work toward the objectives listed in Table 5-1. We will spend the rest of this chapter diving into each of these objectives. If tackling all of this at once is a huge culture shift, start with a few that resonate with you. Then slowly add more activities as your team matures and starts recognizing the benefits.

Table 5-1. *Key objectives for creating a developer pit of success*

Objective
Build a team with a positive/can-do attitude
Ensure requirements and acceptance criteria are understood
Ensure UI design artifacts exist and are understood before starting development
Establish a consistent design identity
Verify the design
Design for testability and design tests
Enable code, build, and test on developer workstations and implement appropriate testing/staging/ production environments
Protect a maker schedule for developers
Ensure every developer has a mentor
Establish clear developer expectations

Positive/Can-Do Team Attitude

If you think back to most of your enjoyable work experiences, it often has little to do with *what* you worked on but everything to do with *who* worked with you. Positive people with can-do attitudes are infectious, and these teams take on challenges and overcome obstacles together.

We must encourage a positive, can-do attitude across the team. Moving from a culture of "manufacturing" software to one of engineering software systems will require significant change and disruption. If every member can bring a positive attitude to problem-solving and team building, they can have a huge impact on the team's ability to overcome obstacles and adopt practices to improve outcomes. The presence of even a single negative team member can destroy a team's ability to move forward.

Ensuring Requirements and Acceptance Criteria Are Understood

Building software is expensive. Building the wrong software and having to rebuild it is doubly expensive. How often have you seen the wrong thing built in a sprint? The developer takes on a task in sprint planning and, at the end of the iteration, demos something that isn't correct. Usually, it isn't a complete rework of what they built, but it was clear they didn't understand the requirements correctly. How often does that happen?

Making sure developers are going to build what is expected is essential to minimizing rework. And it isn't just about minimizing the risk that they build the wrong thing, but also that they build it in the wrong way. Software systems are extremely complex. Having the entire system appear as though it was designed by the same mind is extremely important for minimizing the effort needed to understand how the system works and improving its maintainability.

In Chapter 2, we discussed the danger of hidden assumptions and incomplete pictures, and the importance of developing a shared understanding between stakeholders and the development team. We also shared a variety of lean practices that can help the team uncover the requirements hidden from you and others. As we move closer to development, there will be even more detail that can be uncovered to reveal the "complete picture" shown in Figure 2-6.

Traditionally, when a developer starts diving into implementing a feature story, they primarily rely on their experience and knowledge to manage all of the detailed decisions they end up making every step of the way. They routinely uncover feature scenarios or conditions that were not explicitly discussed or represented in the design artifacts. There are also non-functional requirement decisions that must be made as well. Sometimes they may ask a question of a team member or stakeholder, and sometimes they might just make a unilateral decision and move on. Herein lies another example of small, seemingly innocuous decisions that accumulate over time, erode the quality of the system, and introduce risk of rework. Errors in judgment flourish in an environment where developers of varying skills and experience are allowed to make these types of decisions without any structured critical thought and collaboration with the rest of the team. Ensuring the developers have a firm understanding of what they need to build and how they should build it is critically important. If we don't do this, we are leaving much of our success to chance.

The easiest way to ensure developers have a grip on the requirements is to have them state the requirements back. This will force a lot of critical thought, but doing this early on is better than letting it unfold by accident later in the process. An hour or two spent on a critical thinking activity that helps ensure the developers are heading down the right path is a small price to pay to prevent a lot of rework.

Getting predictable results from this type of activity requires taking a structured approach. We have found consistent success with having developers complete a structured analysis document we call a "whitepaper." This activity guides the developer through a series of seemingly easy questions. Some of the questions are focused on requirements, and some are on the "how." By guiding the developer through these questions, they will be forced to think critically and deeply about what they need to build and how they intend to build it.

This pre-coding critical thinking step will rub some people the wrong way. They will say some tasks are too simple to warrant this level of effort. And they are partially right. Many tasks probably don't warrant this level of effort, but without doing a little analysis, how do you know which ones are too simple to skip? If we are honest with ourselves, we will recognize that we often think tasks are easier than they really are.

It is important to keep this effort lightweight. There is a point of diminishing return with these types of activities. You wouldn't want developers spending weeks on whitepapers each sprint. If you have decomposed requirements into efforts of less than a week (see Chapter 2), you should be able to timebox this effort to one or two hours. If the developer feels they need more than a couple of hours for a whitepaper during a sprint, it is probably a sign of an issue with the definition of the work. Either it is not defined enough, or it is too vague and unclear.

Once the whitepaper document is completed, it should be reviewed by other members of the team. This review step is essential. It is where any hidden assumptions from other members of the team will emerge. Working through these hidden assumptions is essential for putting developers into the pit of success.

Note   Once again, using our house analogy from Chapter 1, the level of design we are doing at this stage is roughly equivalent to the very detailed specifications of how particular details of the house will be constructed. For example, an architect's drawing for the details of the bathroom might omit many details regarding the routing of the plumbing for the room. It will be left to the plumber to analyze the design of the bathroom and determine the best approach to route the plumbing to accommodate the geometry of the existing walls as well as construction code requirements.

The following is a listing and description of the questions we have used in our "whitepaper" analysis document template. You can download this template from the companion website and use it as a starting point for your own version.

What Is My Understanding of the Requirements? What Is the Primary Goal or Objective?

This question is used to articulate, in your own words, the intent of this feature/requirement, and how it is intended to work. Include the desired impact/capability for the intended user or beneficiary of this feature.

What Are the Secondary Goals/Objectives?

List any secondary objectives or goals that are separate from the primary objective.

What Are the Known Design Constraints?

What limitations have been imposed on the implementation of this feature that will impact the design decisions? Constraints can come from a variety of sources: cost, time, hosting, user requirements, performance, etc.

In general, design constraints are a valuable tool to reduce the scope of possible solutions. Identifying these constraints early on can help guide us to the best design decisions.

What Are the Acceptance Criteria for the Solution (Including Non-functional)?

Enumerate the list of criteria by which the success or failure of the implementation should be judged. Be sure to include non-functional criteria such as performance, quality, reliability, resource utilization, etc.

What Assumptions Am I Making About These Requirements and the System?

Often when you are going through this process of analyzing and writing down how you are going to build something, you uncover something you had not considered that must be addressed, even though it is not spelled out in the requirements. For example, if the requirement is "charge the credit card as part of a product fulfillment process," you might ask yourself, "What happens if the attempt to charge the card fails for some reason?" Another assumption might be that you will be able to test this credit card workflow without using a real credit card. This is where you can start listing your assumptions about how you should be handling some of these undocumented requirements so that other stakeholders can review and validate these assumptions.

What Are the Unknowns? (i.e., What Information Is Not Currently Available?)

In addition to uncovering requirements that you can make assumptions about, you might also uncover something that is completely unknown. This can also impact development once you get started. For example, maybe there is an API that you need to use but the definition of that API is not published yet. Or maybe there is an algorithm that needs to be developed, and it is not known if it is even feasible.

What Are the Trade-offs I Am Deliberately Making?

We are always making trade-offs. Most of the time, it feels like these are implicit and not explicit. The goal of this question is to try to get the developer to identify trade-offs they may be making in their approach. Consistency, performance, maintainability, testability, etc.

What Areas/Features Are Most Likely to Change over Time?

As you are analyzing these requirements, it will be important for you to assess what areas of the software are likely to change down the road. These future changes could be the result of user feedback or new feature development. This information will inform how your design should be encapsulating these volatilities.

What Are Anticipated/Possible Failure Scenarios, and How Should They Be Handled?

The purpose of this question is to get you thinking about how the system might behave once you get off the "happy path" of execution. Things to think about here include (but are not limited to)

- What happens if an external dependency (service, API, etc.) fails or does not respond as expected?

- What if inputs to the logic are outside your expectations?

- What if the system comes under an unexpected load?

- Where and how should exceptions be handled?

- If a multi-step process fails at some mid-point, what should the steps be to recovery, completion, and/or return to a consistent state?

- Do you need to use some sort of persisted multi-state flag to determine progress?

- Should you put in some strategic logging to give details when certain failures occur?

- Do you have any potential race conditions?

Are There Any Special Considerations Related to Security?

Do you need to authenticate and/or authorize the user accessing the business logic you are developing? Is there any special treatment of sensitive data that should be taken into account? Are you potentially exposing sensitive data in exception logs, etc.?

What Are the Existing Areas Impacted?

This question is intended to demonstrate identifying the modules/classes/services that are impacted by this feature, along with the types of changes that will be made to these components. This question should also be used to identify the service interface and data contract modifications that will be required.

How Will the Design/Architecture Need to Change?

This question is intended to surface any assumptions you are making about changes to the architecture. Are you adding any new services, classes, modules, etc.? Are you creating any new interfaces or data contracts?

How Can I Encapsulate Current and Future Change?

The purpose of this question is to get you to analyze the current feature/requirement in terms of the likelihood that it will change in the future. The idea is to help you think through what the best approach is for encapsulating future change.

How Should I Test and Validate the System?

What will be your strategy for deciding how to validate that the system performs as expected? Aside from writing unit tests, are there specific integration tests that you will want to develop/modify to verify this requirement? What are some edge cases you will want to make sure you are testing? What regression tests will be required to ensure that there are no unintended changes to the system behavior? Are there any special considerations and requirements in order to effectively validate the system (e.g., special set up/tear down or environmental conditions)?

What Risks Am I Aware Of?

Examples of risk considerations:

- Do you feel there is uncertainty in the outcome of this effort?

- Is there any risk related to the estimates that have been provided?

- Is there a level of requirements ambiguity that could result in significant rework?

- Are you missing any information required to fully understand the requirements (e.g., UI/UX designs/workflows, algorithm specifications, etc.)?

- Are we using new technologies that we are not familiar with?

- Are you concerned about the stability/robustness of technologies or third-party dependencies?

- Do any of the aforementioned assumptions represent a significant risk if they are not valid?

What Concerns Do I Have?

Is there anything else that you can think of that you would want to surface in this document?

What Are the Specific Steps to Implemention, and What Is Their Level of Effort?

The answer to this question will become the sequential plan for implementing this feature/requirement and will include the final estimate of the level of effort to complete each task. These development tasks should be entered into the project management system to track progress during the sprint. In addition to specific feature development tasks, other things to consider here would be

- New/modified data contracts

- New/modified service contracts

- New/modified unit and integration tests

- Manual testing efforts

Key Point   Remember that coding and implementation is the manufacturing phase of software engineering. The developer is assembling the code in such a way that the feature outlined in the user story will be realized. The development of the specific implementation tasks must be focused on identifying the set of sequential activities or steps that the developer will implement as part of this "manufacturing" effort. As an exercise, assume you needed to teach someone to tie their shoe, but you could only do it by describing the specific steps instead of showing them. Try writing down these steps.

UI Design Artifacts Before Development

In the developer life presented earlier, Aaron had to redo much of his user experience work because he didn't implement it as the UI designer had intended. Was the design available when the iteration started? No, the developer guessed how it should look.

When a developer guesses how something should look, we can expect they will make some wrong guesses. For a project that has been established for years, the probability of guessing wrong goes down, as existing styles and patterns are in place, but they still guess wrong more than you would expect. For a greenfield project (new software project) with no or few established patterns, they will frequently guess wrong. Regardless, developers should not have to guess about the design of the UI. This is another example of leaving outcomes to chance.

In Chapter 3, we discussed the critical importance of these UI design artifacts and why these artifacts are often missing at the beginning of development. We also walked through a strategy to avoid these scenarios.

If we want the developer to fall into the pit of success, UI artifacts must exist before an iteration starts.

Design Identity

As we have discussed, software development is a team sport. Software development requires many individuals to work together to build features. Working together is essential. Part of working together is communication, part is having a great attitude, and part is having a shared plan. That is why having a common design identity is essential for developers to fall into the pit of success.

Software is abstract, not a physical thing we can hold in our hands. It is thought up by people and run by computers. But essential in that flow is the communication of that thought between developers. Having a common design identity makes those conversations faster and easier.

There are many ways to solve a problem with software. Many paradigms can be employed. Many technical options could be used. But the more options we consider, the larger the search space becomes for identifying an acceptable solution.

As an example, let's consider a product that has two frameworks for accessing a database: Framework 1 and Framework 2. Each has its own set of advantages and disadvantages. Neither is perfect. But every time a developer wants to access the database, they must choose Framework 1 or Framework 2. Every act becomes a decision. If only one framework was used, there would be no decision to make. Often, the choice between something like frameworks doesn't matter for most solutions.

Deciding between the differences of two frameworks isn't nearly as important as picking the overall architectural style used by a project. Imagine you were building a house, and some of the house had a modern style while other parts were more arts and crafts, and still others were colonial. If a project is an amalgamation of many architectural styles, developers can understandably become paralyzed when having to decide how they should implement their feature.

Software that looks like it was all designed by the same person means the developer has fewer arbitrary decisions to make, and can focus on implementing the feature while maintaining the consistency of the overall design. If there is only one framework for accessing the database, only that one framework will be used. If the system uses a Service Oriented Architecture (SOA), then all the code will look like an SOA system.

This is referred to as conceptual integrity, which is the notion that the design of a system looks consistent throughout as if it had been designed by the same person. You just look at it, and it makes sense.

When building a solution, we recommend you create something that minimizes variations in the following:

- Programming languages

- Frameworks

- Architecture tiers (no more pieces than you need)

- Software taxonomy for the naming of the various types of components in your system

If you have ever worked on a solution that employs many programming languages, you may have encountered a situation where each developer rules their own little fiefdom. Each developer had to make changes to their own area, and no one else could. We don't want a software kingdom of individual fiefdoms; we want systems that look like they were designed and built by a single person.

We also want to minimize the use of frameworks. Every framework added to a solution needs to be carefully considered, and only added if necessary. Each framework added comes with a maintenance burden that you will have to carry for the lifetime of that product. Also, each framework added increases the things a developer needs to know to be successful on that project.

Service-Based Systems

Many design paradigms can result in successful software, but it is important to have a common design identity. We recommend service-based systems because we believe they are often the simplest to understand. They promote loose coupling, making them an excellent choice for building applications in our current environment of cloud-based, distributed computing.

Using services has another benefit; the separation of behavior from data just makes things simpler to understand. In this services model, the services do things but typically have no state. They are passed objects, Data Transfer Objects (DTO), to their methods and perform operations based upon those inputs. This is a very simple software pattern for developers to wrap their heads around.

Another advantage of this separation of behavior and data is that it can often lead to simpler unit testing. Because data objects are separate from the behavior in the services, you only need to test the services. And because the services don't have any properties, they don't have any state to set up when performing the unit test. This makes writing automated tests against services much easier than other programming models like object-oriented.

Choosing a design identity includes choosing a methodology for decomposing and designing your systems, something we discussed in Chapter 4.

Reviewing and Verifying the Design

We want to encourage reviews of work before people take on a bigger chunk of work. Reviewing UI screens before the team starts developing them can save a lot of work. But, if you find yourself needing seven meetings to review those UI screens for final signoff, it might not be worth it.

Things that should be reviewed are things that have a large impact, such as UI designs or architectural designs. But the single biggest impact on a project is the requirements. If you are going to review one thing with your team, review these. Walk through each requirement and the acceptance criteria for that requirement. Make sure everyone knows what we need to build. The next most important item to review is the design artifacts. Review architectural designs and UI designs with the entire team. Make sure everyone knows how we are going to build the system.

Reviewing requirements, acceptance criteria, UI designs, and architectural designs with the team will carry you a long way toward success. It is also important to review detailed designs, especially those that involve how individual services and modules interact. This is where the excessive coupling and poor information hiding will surface, as we discussed in Chapter 4.

Testability

When most people think about testing software, they imagine clicking through the software's user interface. They might imagine having very rigid test plans to click through the user interface. This is often referred to as manual testing, and it should always be done. In addition, developers should also write automated tests. These are tests written in code that test the code.

These automated tests should be part of all software development. When a developer submits their code for a code review, they should include automated tests as part of the work. The developer shouldn't be allowed to submit the final code without automated tests. The exact type of tests may vary depending upon the type of work, but there should be automated tests.

When writing automated tests, developers should generally include two types of tests, unit tests and integration tests. Almost all work submitted in a code review should have a mixture of both types. As a rule of thumb, there should be more unit tests than integration tests.

When fixing bugs, the ideal workflow is to create a new unit test that verifies the bug exists (i.e., the test fails) and then implement the fix such that the test passes. This unit test then becomes a part of the library of tests that are routinely run during automated builds.

Unit tests are important because they allow the developer to test their code without worrying about the surrounding dependencies. Integration tests are important because they *do* run with the external dependencies intact and exercise workflows within the system. Each has a separate purpose. Typically, it is easier to write and maintain many unit tests. Integration tests are usually hard to write, and more time-consuming to maintain. This is a good reason to initially focus on ensuring your most important paths are tested this way.

Tools supporting automated testing have evolved quite rapidly since the introduction of the original xUnit[1] testing frameworks in the 1990s. They are well supported and so easy to use in such a wide variety of development environments, that there really is no excuse for not testing core business logic with automated tests. Some of the more recent advancements like data-driven testing allow us to write a single test and have it iterate

---

[1]www.martinfowler.com/bliki/Xunit.html

over a collection of input parameters and expected results. This greatly reduces the burden of writing separate tests and validations for each combination of input/output conditions.

Deciding What to Unit Test

Forcing developers to write tests will help to ensure the quality of their work, but simply writing a few automated tests alone won't allow them to fall into the pit of success. Developers need strategies for writing their tests. Writing a lot of tests seems like a great idea, but remember, all those tests are more code that needs to be maintained. Creating overlapping or redundant tests should be avoided and can be an indication that there is no formal structure to defining what tests should be written. We will get mixed results from this effort if we allow developers to determine how to test using their own judgment and experience. Like other parts of our process, we want more structured critical thought in test design, so that we have a predictable result that is more consistent across the spectrum of developer skills and experience.

When writing tests for some new functionality, our philosophy should be to get the "biggest bang for our buck" and avoid excessive tests that send us past the point of diminishing return. Ideally, following the 80/20 rule will result in us maximizing our defect detection with the minimum amount of tests. To do this, we need a repeatable, consistent approach to defining our tests that will result in a similar outcome and quality of tests across the development team. Thankfully, lightweight tools and strategies already exist to provide this structured approach. In Chapter 22 of his book *Code Complete*,[2] Steve McConnell provides details of an approach that layers a series of existing test analysis approaches to create insights into what needs to be tested, and results in an optimized list of detailed test scenarios for a software method or function.

Combining three of the analysis techniques McConnell covers, (1) basis testing, (2) data flow testing, and (3) boundary checking, is a good starting point for creating a disciplined approach to automated test design. Table 5-2 shows the resulting test matrix from the analysis of the code shown in Listing 5-1 that determines an employee's eligibility for two types of bonuses.

---

[2]McConnell, Steven C. 2004. *Code Complete*, 2nd ed. Microsoft Press.

Listing 5-1. Method to compute employee bonus

```
public int ComputeEmployeeBonus(int employeeId)
{
        // Compute the total bonus for an employee

        int basicBonus = 0;

        // compute basic bonus for full-time low wage
        // earners
        if (_employees[employeeId].IsFullTime &&
           _employees[employeeId].Salary < MaxBaseSalary)
        {
            basicBonus = ComputeBasicBonus(employeeId);
        }

        int performanceBonus = 0;

        // compute performance bonus
        if (_employees[employeeId].IsPerformanceEligible)
        {
            performanceBonus =
                ComputePerformanceBonus(employeeId,
                                    basicBonus);
        }

        return basicBonus + performanceBonus;
}
```

Table 5-2. *Test matrix following basis testing, data flow testing, and boundary checking analysis*

Test	Scenario	Description	Full Time?	Salary	Eligible for Performance Bonus?
1	Nominal case	All "if" conditions true	Yes	Max − 1	Yes
2	1st "if" false because 1st condition false	Employee is not full time, salary < max	No	Max − 1	Yes
3	1st "if" false because 2nd condition false	Employee is not full time, salary >= max	Yes	Max + 1	Yes
4	2nd "if" false	Employee not performance eligible	Yes	Max − 1	No
5	Define `basicBonus` on line 22 and first use on line 38	Employee is not full time and is not performance eligible	No	Max − 1	No
6	Salary directly on the `MaxBaseSalary` boundary	Employee is full time, salary = max	Yes	Max	Yes

Isolating Developer Environments

The ability to test code quickly and easily is essential to successful development. If developers can't test things locally on their own machines, they will not be very successful. They will struggle to make forward progress. When a developer makes a change, they must be able to test the change easily.

Developers must be able to work independently and be able to run the entire solution, including the automated tests, on their machine. This is a key part of the pit of success. If a developer breaks the build because of a broken automated test, they should be able to run that test on their machine and replicate the issue. If someone finds a bug in the QA or production environments, the developer needs the ability to reproduce the issue on their machine. This is an often-overlooked part of a successful development setup. It is worthwhile to design a system and choose technologies that allow a developer to develop and test locally.

That leads to another key for successful development, excellent environments. All software products need to have testing, staging, and production environments. The testing environments need to run the latest code merged into the master branch. This gives developers and test professionals a chance to verify code before it goes to production. These environments should be paired with staging and production environments (see Figure 5-2). Staging is almost a clone of production but runs the latest code (staging might be optional for a beta/MVP release of a product). Production is the latest version being accessed by actual customers.

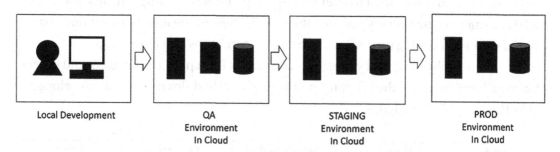

Figure 5-2. *Recommended environments to support development*

Having these environments is only part of the puzzle. All builds and deployments to these environments should be automated. No human should have to manually do builds or manually copy files around to build applications for these environments. Builds should be automated. Having this in place will reduce the burden on developers for successful releases and reduce human error.

Maker Schedule

Developers need to have the time necessary to complete the work assigned to them. In many organizations, developers' days are cut up into a series of 30-minute blocks. It is difficult to get much done in 30 minutes when your job is to design and build something. Software development is a tough challenge; you need large windows of time to achieve success. Ideally, try and create three to four-hour blocks for developers to dive into problems.

As we showed in the Developer Life story earlier, Aaron's schedule is a mess. He doesn't have open blocks of time to write software. Instead, he fits software development into small windows of time. Software venture capitalist Paul Graham wrote on this topic called "Maker's Schedules, Manager's Schedules."[3] He compared and contrasted the schedule needs of someone whose job is to create (i.e., the Maker) vs. someone whose job is to manage (i.e., the Manager).

The Maker schedule needs long open blocks of time to solve hard problems. If a developer is planning on working from 8:00 a.m. to noon, that would be a nice four-hour block of time. But if someone schedules a one-hour meeting at 10:00 a.m., the developer has two small blocks of time that won't be as effective. The first two-hour block will probably be partly consumed waiting for the 10:00 a.m. meeting. The open block from 11:00 a.m. to noon is too small to attempt any deep problem-solving. The insertion of the 10:00 a.m. meeting has greatly reduced the effectiveness of the four-hour window. Four potential hours of coding turned into a couple of start/stops and a meeting.

It may be challenging, and you may get pushback from project managers and others. However, it will be worth the effort to transform your schedules to give your developers a calendar that looks like Figure 5-3.

Monday	Tuesday	Wednesday	Thursday	Friday
	Standup	Standup	Standup	Standup
Iteration Planning	Focus time	Focus time	Focus time	Focus time
Lunch	Lunch	Lunch	Lunch	Lunch
Focus time	Focus time	Focus time	Cross Team Developer Pre-Planning	Focus time
Code Review	Code Review	Code Review	Code Review	Code Review

Figure 5-3. *Example of a healthy Maker schedule*

---

[3]`www.paulgraham.com/makersschedule.html`

Mentor

Every developer needs to have a mentor they trust and then meet with them regularly. Software development is a team sport, and everyone must be engaged and working to continue to improve. Most developers suffer from some level of impostor syndrome, so staying connected to someone they look up to can help build their confidence and keep them moving forward in their professional development.

Development can be very difficult and challenging. A mentor is someone that developers can rely upon for honest feedback, both positive and negative, which is essential. Having someone to discuss challenges, express frustrations, and get general guidance from is critical in such a demanding field.

Establishing Clear Developer Expectations

Developers can play a huge part in their own success, but it is important that they clearly know what is expected from them. They can't achieve expectations that are vague, or that they don't know or understand. There are many activities developers do to ensure success, such as creating whitepapers for each assigned activity and getting work done for each iteration. These specific responsibilities for developers need to be spelled out and understood by the team. Table 5-3 shows an example of the clear expectations for developers on a team.

Table 5-3. *Example of setting clear developer expectations*

Expectation	What it means
Meet your commitments	Each sprint is a commitment of the work to be completed by an engineer. Follow through and complete that work by the end of the sprint. It's never okay to miss a commitment. Hold others accountable to their commitments.
Apply critical thought	Critical thinking activities are assigned with every activity assigned to a developer in a sprint. These may include Design analysis, detailed design, UI task decomposition, and testing requirements.

(continued)

Table 5-3. (*continued*)

Expectation	What it means
Create tasks for your work	All work items (stories/activities) are tasked out to represent the sequential steps to be finished to complete the work.
Demand acceptance criteria	Acceptance criteria are written for all stories/activities that require it. Developers need to demand the criteria when they are not provided.
Get approval for interface and data contract changes	Any changes/additions to Interfaces or DTOs should be included in critical thinking documentation and reviewed by the development lead before implementation.
Implement the UI as designed	Developers are expected to implement the UI as designed. Schedule time with the UI designer (if needed) to review design aspects that have implementation challenges. Any challenges should be brought to the development lead and worked out with the UI/UX team.
Take ownership of estimates and effort	Developers need to be aware of the estimate for the work item and are accountable for seeking help when the effort will exceed the estimate. This must be done with sufficient estimate remaining so that timely help can be provided, and the work item has a chance of being completed close to the estimate.
Seek help when needed	As a general guideline, developers will not spend more than an hour struggling with a problem without seeking help. There needs to be an effort made before seeking help.
Provide effective updates	Developers need to give updates that proactively and clearly communicate challenges, issues, and concerns so that assistance can be provided and expectations and adjustments can be addressed. If encountering a roadblock, come to standup with a proposed plan(s) or next step(s) for overcoming the roadblock.
Design effective unit tests	Unit tests are designed and implemented using basis, data flow, and bounds testing analysis as a minimum.
Design effective integration tests	Developers need to focus on the correct integration tests for the activity assigned.

(*continued*)

Table 5-3. (*continued*)

Expectation	What it means
Determine necessary regression testing	Developers need to consider the potential for unintended behavior because of their changes and identify and execute the appropriate regression tests.
Thorough verification before marking tasks done	All tasks considered complete are given reasonable manual testing prior to submitting, which includes verifying all acceptance criteria.
Review completed UI tasks with UI designer	Once the developer has implemented code for a UI, they will need to take screen captures or videos of the critical views and share them with the UI designer for review.
Code demos should reflect finished work	End of sprint should include a demo that means code is done, code reviewed, merged, deployed, and working in the QA environment.
Keep code review submissions small	Strive for code review submissions that are fewer than 200–400 lines of code changes.

Pit of Success Checklist

The following is a checklist of the key activities we have outlined in our description of what it will take to ensure developers are regularly falling into the pit of success:

- Are whitepapers being used?

- Are UI artifacts available before development?

- Do sprints/iterations begin with the dependencies completed?

- Is there a common design pattern?

- Are design reviews occurring?

- Are developers writing automated tests as they write the code?

- Are code reviews occurring?

- Do developers have a structured process for designing their tests?

- Are developers able to effectively build, test, and debug from their own machines?

- Do developers have a maker's schedule?

- Can developers work independently?

- Are demos occurring from a QA/Test environment?

- Does everyone have a mentor?

- Are the expectations for developers clear?

Summary

Designing for success is not accidental, and neither is the plan for the workday of a developer. The day needs to be engineered to ensure developers fall into the pit of success more often than not. This requires actively managing all aspects of the development phase by implementing structures, processes, and expectations. This allows us to identify and correct errors in judgment that will lead to rework.

Key Takeaways

- **Constraints will help reduce the solution space** for developers.

- **Design reviews and design handoffs ensure everyone understands** what we are building and how we intend to build it.

- **Developer-driven design documents reduce rework and increase shared understanding**. Using structured tools enable them to think things through without having to think on the spot in a meeting or while coding.

- **Having completed UI design and good acceptance criteria** reduces guesswork by the developer.

- **Designs that have conceptual integrity are simpler** for developers to comprehend and maintain.

- **Service-based systems are easier for developers to reason about**.

- **Ensuring the system is testable** allows developers to develop confidently.

- **A disciplined approach to designing automated tests** will increase their effectiveness at defect detection.

- **Developers should be able to build, debug, and test independently**.

- **It is important to get developers on a maker schedule**, not a manager schedule.

- **Have a mentor relationship for each developer** in your organization.

- **Establishing clear expectations for developers** will help them understand what success will look like for them.

Now that we have given our developers the support they need to be successful, we can turn our attention to what will be required to establish quality as a core value within the organization.

CHAPTER 6

Institutionalized Quality

Introduction

There is no silver bullet to quality in software development. Quality must be valued throughout an organization so that quality practices can exist at all levels and in all processes. In this chapter, we will focus on key practices that will help ensure quality throughout the entire process.

Reality Check

Have you ever had a water leak in your home? All it takes is one small flaw, and the water finds its way out. Quality in software is a lot like plumbing; each piece must be working. Any small defect in a software system can result in system failures and bad experiences for users.

Imagine if you had built a software platform used by a variety of customers. Your software platform lives in multiple locations, and communications between these locations are secured using certificates. The certificates will need to be verified; they will expire at some point. Then imagine your code contains flawed date checking logic that does not correctly handle date math. When attempting to verify your certificate you would have an invalid date, and it would fail the validation. The failed validation would stop communication between your locations, and your service would go down. And most importantly, you'd have unhappy customers, all because of a little bit of math. Trust me, this sort of thing can and does happen.[1]

---

[1] www.wired.com/2012/03/azure-leap-year-bug/

© Doug Durham and Chad Michel 2021
D. Durham and C. Michel, *Lean Software Systems Engineering for Developers*,
https://doi.org/10.1007/978-1-4842-6933-6_6

The other big challenge for quality is moving fast. Software development moves very quickly. We all try to deliver features at a rapid pace. Business goals are dependent upon software releases, so delaying those releases is painful to the organization. There will be pressure to deliver quickly. Often, shortcuts are taken in the processes and practices that help ensure you meet your quality objectives. It is easy to understand how these decisions are rationalized. It can be difficult for people and organizations to prioritize something abstract such as quality in the absence of known quality issues (i.e., known defects). Only after the end-user identifies defects do we second-guess our decision to cut corners during development.

The bottom line is there are significant challenges related to quality that are pervasive in our industry. Since 2009, CapGemini has produced, almost annually, a *World Quality Report*[2] that contains the results of a market research study exploring a variety of dimensions in software quality. The 12th edition of this report (*World Quality Report* 2020-21) contained the following findings:

- 58% of respondents indicated they had enough time for testing.

- 45% say they have the right testing strategy/process/methodology.

- 69% are meeting their quality goals.

- 99% are having difficulties testing in an agile environment.

Moving Fast vs. Maintaining a Rapid Pace

There is a natural tendency to view quality as the opposite of speed. They say you can move fast or you can move confidently with quality. It is a false dichotomy. What if the reality is you can't move fast *without* quality?

In Chapter 4, we discussed Martin Fowler's "Design Stamina Hypothesis,"[3] where he argues that you can move faster for a short period without design. But over time, it will be hard to keep adding features to a system without a good design. Over the long term, spending some time on design will allow you to move faster. Design isn't the only way to focus on quality, but it is a big component. Fowler's argument in the design stamina hypothesis makes intuitive sense and is something we have experienced first-hand.

---

[2] www.worldqualityreport.com

[3] https://martinfowler.com/bliki/DesignStaminaHypothesis.html

If we know that it makes sense to spend a little bit of time doing design, why do so many development teams insist on avoiding design? The same question applies to the adoption of quality practices. Why is there pushback?

Ultimately, we are making a trade-off, speed now for lack of speed in the future. We choose to achieve our immediate goals, knowing deep down it sacrifices our goals in the future.

When we prioritize short-term speed over long-term stability, we open ourselves to the risk of major defects and issues in our software. Major issues would be issues with the software that prevents a core scenario from functioning. All software will have some issues, and it is important to delineate between major and minor issues. Our goal should be to prevent all major issues from ever reaching the hands of a customer. Here is another way to look at it: major issues require development teams to stop work and immediately fix the issue because customers are being impacted. Sometimes this is referred to as a showstopper.

Working on a poor-quality product with major issues is hard. Just ask any developer that has experienced this. Products that have chronic major defects complicate forward progress. The continual interruption these defects create derails each sprint.

Derailing delivery of work in a sprint is a red flag for everyone on a team. It will occasionally happen, but it shouldn't be the norm. If you are going to deliver software quickly, then each sprint needs to be successful. If we can't complete a small section of our work on time, how can we expect to complete larger sections of work on time?

Toward an Integrated, Layered View

Throughout the previous chapters, we have discussed various tools, techniques, and processes that will improve the quality of the outcomes of our development efforts. Given the critical role that these efforts play in our desired outcomes as well as just our personal satisfaction (something we will touch on more in Chapter 8), we felt it was important to dedicate a chapter to this topic to emphasize the importance and allow us to create a clear picture of the integrated, layered approach to quality that is necessary. It also allows us to introduce some additional quality practices that we have not had a chance to discuss yet.

Quality Targets

It's important to have goals and ways to measure our progress. Whether it is a time you are trying to achieve in running a marathon or a certain level in a martial art, having something we can objectively measure our progress against helps us with focus and determination. It also helps us determine whether what we are doing to achieve these goals is making a difference.

Quality is no different. We can't just say we want to create quality software. We must be able to measure something to determine how we are doing and how we compare to benchmarks from our industry. One of the challenges is that the overall quality of a piece of software is a difficult thing to assert. There is no one metric that determines the level of quality, no one score. Part of the problem is that there are many dimensions to software quality beyond things like defects. Some of these dimensions are usability, feature set, and customer satisfaction.

The other challenge with metrics is that they must constructively shape our behavior and align with our overall objectives. When you start measuring something in an organization, people will naturally make choices that positively impact what is being measured. If we were to count lines of code to measure productivity, would there be any doubt people would start writing more code than usual? We may not get more real output (i.e., features), but we will definitely get more lines of code.

We have settled on two key metrics and targets that have worked well to both measure our progress and shape the behaviors of our teams: defect detection rate and percentage of rework.

Defect Detection Rate

Defect detection rate is an indicator of quality process effectiveness and is defined as the percentage of all defects identified by internal quality practices. This metric is calculated by dividing the number of bugs found internally by the total number of bugs found. A good rule of thumb is to have a defect detection rate target of around 90%-95%. This would imply our processes effectively find 90%-95% of the defects in our system before it goes to production. The customers or end-users are the ones who are finding the other 5%-10%.

Key Point   Defect detection rate = Bugs found internally / All bugs found

---

When tracking this metric, it is important to have a rolling window of data as opposed to continuing to calculate the metric for all data, all of the time. The trend is as important as the actual metric. As a starting point, only calculate the metric for all bugs found in the previous three or four months. This gives you a pretty good indicator of how you are currently doing and enables you to compare against prior periods to see if you are getting better or worse over time.

Another key point is to track information that will allow you to examine the source of the defects you are finding. As you continue to adjust your quality practices, you will want to have some data to support the rationale for changes you are making and to be able to determine the effectiveness of these changes.

Finally, the timing of when something is considered a bug is also important. A defect that is discovered by the developer as they are testing their work, as part of completing their task, is not a defect to be tracked. In general, defects should only be tracked when they are found after a developer has submitted their work to be merged into the main code base. In other words, once the developer feels they are done with the task, and no further effort should be required of them, defects can begin to be tracked.

Percentage of Rework

Percentage of rework is an indicator of team productivity. Rework is defined as development tasks and defect fixes resulting from releasing a feature we felt was complete, but find out later that it is not acceptable to our clients or stakeholders. All defects are, by definition, rework, but not all rework is classified as a defect. The software could be working exactly as it was meant to, but there was a miscommunication at the requirement level. Not all software teams would classify this as a defect, but it is most definitely rework.

Rework is not concerned with the count of items but with the amount of time spent working on items that are considered rework. The metric is calculated by dividing the amount of effort spent on tasks that are classified as rework by the total amount of effort by the development team. Comparing this metric against some rough benchmarks will give you an idea of how well you are doing:

- Above average: rework percentages < 50%

- Very good: rework percentages < 25%

- Outstanding: rework percentages < 10%

Key Point   Percentage of rework = (Effort spent on rework / All effort) × 100

It is not necessary to have fine-grained time tracking to get value out of this metric. For example, it would be acceptable at the end of each week to ask each developer how much time they spent on the tasks labeled as rework and then divide the total of those times by the number of developers multiplied by 40 hours. As with defect detection, we also want to use a rolling window for this metric to see how we are currently doing and how we compare to historical trends. We also want to have some additional information about the source of the rework for analysis and process changes.

Quality Mindset

Quality affects everyone on a project. Constant interruptions from quality issues are a huge problem with teams. But quality isn't just about bugs. Reworking code because of comments from a code review also impacts the project. Reworking a system's architecture because the architecture doesn't support the current features is a major undertaking and most certainly causes us to move slower.

Quality can't be the focus of only one person. It is too important. Everyone must be focused on quality, all the time. Quality needs to be seen as a primary goal from the top and have leadership support, even when schedules are tight and there is pressure to cut corners. While individual developers have a significant impact on the quality of a product, the technical leads, architects, project managers, and product owners also have significant roles to play in ensuring the level of quality.

Not only does everyone need to have a focus on quality, but they need to be focused on finding issues, not verification. You can never really prove that software works, but you *can* prove that it doesn't work. Let's make an analogy to illustrate this. A handful of pennies is on the bottom of a big swimming pool, like a handful of bugs might be in your code. How would we prove that there are *not* any pennies in the pool? We would have to scan the entire floor of the pool inch by inch. By the time we got to the far edge of the pool, we might wonder, is there one back at the start that was added since I looked there? Proving that there *is* a penny in the pool is easier. All we have to do is find *one*. If we know where people have been hanging around in the pool, we can make some good guesses on where to look first.

Finding defects is similar. Proving that there are no defects is difficult. Proving that there is a defect is a more possible outcome, and we can use our intuition and some structured thinking (see Chapter 5) to make it easier to know where to focus. We can find defects, but we can't find or prove that there are no defects. This means that when we are focusing on a quality practice, we should literally be trying to break the software instead of demonstrating that it works.

Key Point   People with a proper quality mindset are constantly looking for ways to "break" the software.

Determining if there is an issue isn't the only important thing. The sooner we can find the issue, the better. Having a customer find an issue in production is costly from a variety of perspectives. First, it is embarrassing for the company and can be damaging to the reputation of the product. Second, they often require immediate action on the part of the development team, and this distracts them from their assigned work. Third, the later an issue is found (especially if it is related to requirements, design, or architecture), the more potential rework will be required to fix it. If the rework is found during a code review, it isn't as expensive to fix as it would be six months later, after more code depends on that code and users are using the system.

Quality Practices Review

Many software organizations still rely primarily on manual testing at the end of the development phase for their quality practice. As we have discussed, quality cannot be achieved with any single practice. There are a number of proven quality practices out there, and each helps to improve the quality of the software product in some way. The bottom line is no single practice can get us to the quality targets we proposed earlier. Layering these practices throughout our development process can minimize the defects, like how layering many semi-transparent sheets of material will eventually prevent any light from passing through.

The rest of this chapter will provide an overview of these layered quality practices organized by the general activities that occur during the software development phase: requirements analysis, design, development, and acceptance testing. Some of this discussion will refer to topics we have discussed in other chapters, and some will be new practices we are introducing here. The goal is to provide a mental model of how we can integrate different activities throughout development to achieve the defect detection and rework targets we have established.

During Requirements Analysis

The first quality practice is the creation of good requirements. Starting with good requirements means the rest of the quality practices will be more effective. Good requirements don't mean perfect requirements, and they also don't mean that the requirements can't change.

Probably one of the most important aspects of requirements is that they are complete for all known use cases for the system. Missing functionality, such as, "we may need to support SMS notifications, not just email" is something we want to identify before moving into design and development activities.

Shared Understanding

In Chapter 2, we discussed the importance of having a shared understanding between stakeholders and the development team and the need to uncover requirements that are knowable but have not been formally identified. The key quality practices we outlined were the use of some lean approaches to visualizing the complete end-user experience through journey maps, and the structured approach to feature backlog development using story maps. We also covered the use of estimation to identify and reduce uncertainty in our collective understanding of the requirements.

Validation of the UI

In Chapter 3, we turned our attention to the use of UI tools and processes to further understand not only what is required but how the system should be built to satisfy the requirements. The development of testable acceptance criteria by product owners will help them think through exact scenarios that can be used to create integration tests and manual testing during development. Gradually refining the level of detail in the UI designs and seeking feedback and approval along the way, with both stakeholders and developers, will help ensure we are aligned with what we need to build.

These investments in good, well understood, and thorough requirements for our software will have a dramatic impact on the reduction of rework later in development.

During Design

Poor requirements and poor design tend to be the hardest problems to fix in a system. Establishing a UI design that satisfies stakeholders and a system design that satisfies the current and future requirements is our objective. There is also the consideration of how we design the execution of the project in order to prioritize work based upon dependencies, risk, and other factors.

Validation of the UI

Chapter 3's focus was not only on making sure the UI meets the needs of the customer but also that the design was understood by developers and reflected their feedback on the feasibility and ease of build.

Another consideration discussed in this chapter is whether it might be possible to accelerate the end-user feedback on a working UI by prioritizing the development of the UI over the development of the supporting back-end services. Getting end-user validation of the actual working UI prior to developing back-end services can reduce rework on these services and increase our confidence in the stability of the API requirements for the services.

Designing Systems That Age Well

Chapter 4 was dedicated to helping avoid the massive slow-down in productivity and eventual re-implementation (i.e., rework) of systems that are not designed for change. Nothing will be more disruptive to a development team and organization than having to start over and rebuild a system because it became unmaintainable.

Along with avoiding the rework of a rewrite, there are other outcomes of having a mature design methodology that contribute to a reduction in defects. Specifically, making it easier for developers to comprehend the system and its design, and reducing their field of view by effective encapsulation of changes. These will reduce the possibility of introducing unintended behaviors in other parts of the system as we are making changes.

Designing How to Execute the Project

Designing how to execute the project is the process of determining the order and assignment of work. This is particularly important when starting a greenfield project (e.g., new systems or applications). This is one of the most underutilized processes in software development and is also one of the most important. Without some critical thought, projects will often sequence work in ways that will cause work to stall as developers wait on other dependencies. The impact of developers waiting on other developers is equivalent to the impact of rework. This should be considered a failure in quality.

Another outcome of poor project execution planning might be that areas of particular risk may be deferred to later in the project. Deferring risk on software projects can result in redesigns and rework if our assumptions about the feasibility do not hold up. Examples might be the use of a third-party API for some part of the system. If the API does not operate as expected, it might require changes to the design or even the requirements. Validating API assumptions prior to development is a good quality practice.

Another aspect of project execution design is identifying checkpoints to measure progress against. It is best to carve up bigger releases into smaller chunks if possible and push these smaller chunks to production as you can. This constant pushing of new features to production will enable faster delivery of features and reduce rework of those features. Instead of delivering ten features in ten months, try delivering one feature each month for ten months. This might not always be possible but, if you can, find ways to make more bite-sized releases. Doing so will minimize your overall risk.

We do not go into detail in this book on best practices for designing project executions. As with choosing a design methodology (Chapter 4), we recommend investigating methodologies that are out there and look for ones that address the quality challenges we have listed here. We would again recommend *Righting Software*,[4] which contains an entire section on project design and provides a prescriptive approach to managing cost and schedule risk.

During Development

As we discussed in Chapter 5, if we can keep developers falling into the pit of success, we can avoid errors in judgment and the ensuing rework to correct defects or implement missing requirements. We then introduced a number of key objectives that aid in

---

[4]Löwy, Juval. 2020. *Righting Software*. Addison-Wesley Professional.

reducing defects and rework that occur during development. Quality processes in this phase are also critical to the preservation of the quality of the overall design of the system.

Establishing Clear Developer Expectations

One of the key objectives in Chapter 5 related to quality was the establishment of clear developer expectations. Specifically, developers must understand their responsibilities. This involves using critical thought, demanding quality requirements and acceptance criteria, testing, and getting feedback on their designs and assumptions. The developers are the last line of defense to prevent errors in judgment in the construction of the software.

Reviewing the Requirements and Design Artifacts

Another key objective in Chapter 5 was taking the time to review the UI and architectural design artifacts to ensure they are understood by the development team. Creating dedicated space and time for developers to really focus on these artifacts will give them a chance to identify areas they are unsure about and ask questions before starting development.

Ensuring Requirements and Acceptance Criteria Are Understood

In Chapter 5, we introduced the use of a document template we called a whitepaper that can be used to help achieve a shared understanding at the detailed implementation level. These whitepapers provide a structured process for a developer to follow that allows them to target their critical thinking about what they need to build, how they need to build it, and how they will approach defect detection and testing. The sharing of this document with stakeholders and technical leads provides an opportunity to course-correct the developer prior to coding.

Enabling a Testable System

Two key objectives in Chapter 5 addressed impacting the ability to effectively test the software we are building. The first is to invest in building automated tests at both the unit and integration levels. Essential to building these automated tests is the need to have a process that developers can use to design the minimum number of tests that should be built that provide the highest likelihood of detecting defects.

The second key objective was enabling developers to easily run both automated and manual tests from their local machines. Removing the friction of testing will promote more testing.

Implementing Continuous Integration with Automated Integration and Unit Tests

The adoption of modern continuous integration tools into our development processes has transformed the developer experience in ways that are hard to overstate. Before, when a developer completed a body of work and submitted a set of code changes to have it reviewed, the reviewer would need to download the branch with the code changes, run a build, and verify that the build succeeds and the tests pass. This was before they even began their code review.

It's easy to say your code works when it is only tested on your machine (a.k.a. WOMM – Works On My Machine). Showing that it runs just as well on the build server is something else entirely. Testing at different milestones along the way instills confidence in your code and your whole system.

With the use of continuous integration tools and pipelines, we can require that a developer's changes are automatically validated against the test suite before a reviewer needs to spend any time reviewing the changes. If the build fails or all tests do not pass, the developer must resolve the issues before considering their changes ready for code review.

Putting off testing until several merges have been completed can set off a proverbial snowball of problems rolling down the hill, and it's a snowball that nobody knows exists until it's too late. By taking the time to automate testing on your build server, you can stop the snowball and prevent your system from becoming the one that nobody wants to work on (and we've all worked on those before).

Using Structured Code Reviews and Pull Requests

Code reviews, especially when they follow a structured approach, are probably the single best activity we can do for the quality of our systems. Much like proofreading a document, you often find problems with how your system was constructed or identify items missing when you go back through it.

The first code review that should be done is a developer desk check. Before a developer submits their changes for review, they should walk through the code on their machine in the debugger, stepping over each line one at a time. This simple practice will find a lot of issues and find them before involving others, which will save time and effort.

The second code review should be done by the lead engineer for the project. Ideally, this code review is initiated using something called a pull request (PR for short). This is a method for submitting finished work for review, approval, and merging into the main code branch of a project. Once the developer has completed their desk check, they can create a pull request in their source control system. Assuming the team has implemented the earlier continuous integration recommendations, this action will start a build and test cycle to verify that the changed code can be merged and passes all build and test activities.

Once the pull request passes the automated validation, the lead engineer can review the submitted pull request. This review of the code should ensure the code will function correctly per the design and requirements. Another, maybe more important part of this review is ensuring the software architecture design was not violated or broken by the changes made by the developer.

It is important to have a checklist to use as part of the code review. This ensures that the developers understand what to expect from the code review and ensures consistency across the code reviews. Think of this checklist like the checklist a pilot uses before takeoff. You know they have taken off hundreds of times, but they still don't rely just on their memory for the preflight activities. Remember, leave nothing to chance. The following is an example of a checklist we have used in our own code reviews.

Pull Request Code Review Checklist

The reviewers of this pull request will verify that the following conditions have been met. Note to developers: please review the first section to make sure you have included everything before submitting the pull request.

Review Before Submitting

- Your code builds clean without any errors or warnings
- PR is small enough to be effectively reviewed (less than 200–400 lines of reviewable code)
- Assign the necessary reviewers to the PR
- Assign corresponding Stories and Activities
- Attach Screenshots of developed UI

Testing

- Appropriate Unit Tests were created with the code

- Appropriate Integration Tests were added if crossing services

- Appropriate UI Tests were created where needed

- Code coverage was maintained

- All tests pass!!!

Architecture

- New services have not been added that weren't in the architecture

- Functionality added to existing services belongs in that service

- There are no references that contradict architecture guidelines

- Business logic is being properly encapsulated and tested

- UI calls to back-end APIs are not too chatty or chunky

- Services are not directly referenced (Only through dependency injection or service calls) Reference abstractions, not the concrete types

- Business volatilities are properly encapsulated (Minimal coupling, High cohesion, and Information Hiding)

- New methods on contracts followed Detailed Design

- Breaking changes have been identified for contracts

- New Data Contracts followed Detailed Design

- No behavior being passed between layers, Data Contracts are only data

- Contracts are being mapped properly between layers

General Code Review

- Code format/styling/casing follows defined coding standards

- Configuration file changes are correct

- No secure credentials are stored in the source code

- Code is self-documenting
- User Variable Names
- Comments
- One class, data structure, interface, or enum per file
- Exceptions are handled properly
- Logging has been added to new code
- New external libraries have the proper license
- New external libraries are encapsulated correctly
- Existing frameworks are on the latest stable version where possible

New Projects

- Namespacing is correct
- New Project belongs in this solution
- Code belongs in a new project and not an existing project

Database Changes

- Upgrade Scripts account for all code changes
- Data types for new fields are correct
- No logic was added to the database that belongs in the code
- No scalability concerns exist for new data
- Indexes are properly defined
- Foreign Keys are properly defined

UI Changes

- Design comps were followed
- The client-side architecture was followed

Cloud Architecture Changes

- New cloud services have been provisioned

- New cloud services are secured

- Release pipeline was updated to deploy new services

Another review could take place before the pull request is merged, where the UI designer would walk through the UI with the developer to ensure it meets the design specs. It is important at this phase to decide what you will consider a major defect that would stop the pull request from being accepted. It is often best not to allow every minor UI display issue to block the pull request. That said, if you are creating a system for consumers (i.e., not internal business customers), your standards here might need to be very high.

During Acceptance Testing and QA Testing

The last quality practice we will discuss is a quality assurance review in the QA environment. This review should walk through all of the acceptance criteria created by the product owner and make sure those requirements work. This review should also ensure that the UI closely mimics the designs created by the UI team. It is not necessary for this to be an exhaustive test. Remember, at this point, the developer should have tested the code, the lead engineer should have reviewed it, and the UI team should have looked over the implemented UI.

Summary

Quality is not something we do at the end of the project. We need to take an integrated, layered approach if we are going to achieve the quality metrics we should be targeting. Every step of the way, we need to be looking for ways to fill gaps in our process that result in the errors in judgment that lead to rework and defects.

Key Takeaways

- **We must improve the quality of our designs and our outputs if we want to move at a constant, rapid pace**.

- **No individual quality practice will enable us to achieve our quality goals**. It will require layering multiple practices throughout the development.

- **It is important to have metrics** to measure the effects of our quality practices.

- **Defect detection rate** will tell us how effective we are at preventing defects from getting to the customer.

- **Percentage of rework** will tell us how much time we are spending addressing quality issues.

- **Quality practices should be a part of requirements analysis, design, development, and acceptance testing**.

- **Designing how a project is executed** will help ensure that developers stay productive and prioritize risky areas.

- **Modern continuous integration tools help automate key quality activities.**

- **Using a structured code review** will help ensure the consistency of this valuable quality practice.

We have now completed our discussion of the five key outcomes that we outlined in Chapter 1:

- Shared understanding across the development team and stakeholders

- Validate user experience early and often

- Software design that ages well

- Developers falling into the pit of success

- Institutionalized quality

There is one more topic that needs our attention before we bring everything together in Chapter 8. That is the topic of introducing a new role on development teams, which is what we will cover in the next chapter.

CHAPTER 7

The Role of Chief Engineer

Introduction

Software development is very technical, with many technical decisions along the journey. These decisions rarely cause massive failures in isolation. As discussed in Chapter 4, it is the sum of many small decisions that often leads to unmaintainable products. Transforming a team into an engine for modern application development will not be possible without a passionate, strong leader who can convince everyone of the better way and then actively works to ensure the team stays on track. This leader needs to be rigorous about insisting on no compromises when it comes to the processes and principles that will achieve these cultural changes and recognizes the risks when outcomes are left to chance. In this chapter, we will focus on the importance of having strong technical leadership within an organization to help nurture and sustain the design and development of our software systems.

Revisiting the Football Analogy

In Chapter 1, we used football as an analogy for the increasing level of complexity we are dealing with in modern application development. It is like moving from youth football to college football. Even though the fundamental concepts of the game are the same, we can't use the same tools and processes learned in youth football and expect to be successful at these higher competition levels.

© Doug Durham and Chad Michel 2021
D. Durham and C. Michel, *Lean Software Systems Engineering for Developers*,
https://doi.org/10.1007/978-1-4842-6933-6_7

We'd like to revisit this same analogy but now from a leadership standpoint. Imagine you have assembled a new team of talented college-level football players, all from different schools. Each of these players has experience playing the game, has had success on previous teams, and understands core concepts of strategy, teamwork, technique, etc. They have watched quite a bit of football and have seen how high-performing teams and players have played. They probably have some athletes they look up to and aspire to emulate on the field.

Now imagine you took these players, sat them down on a Monday, and told them they would be playing against the University of Nebraska on Saturday. They need to do whatever they need to do to get ready, and oh, by the way, there is no coaching staff. Could you imagine the result? At times you might see something that resembled football but, in general, it would look chaotic. Despite having similar player talent, Nebraska would absolutely pummel them. Why? The quality of coaching at Nebraska enables them to play as a team and within the context and vision of how they execute their offense and defense. Without any clear vision, concept, or plan for offense and defense, our team would likely look like 11 individuals who are not on the same page – which is what they are.

Now, imagine you took a group of talented programmers with similar levels of experience and understanding and did the same thing – had them tackle a complicated system to design, build, and maintain. Software development is a team sport, and without an experienced leader or coach with a clear vision who can get the team performing together and within the constraints of the design of the system, you will get a system that looks like it contained the designs and ideas of everyone on the team – in other words, chaos.

Not every football coach can be successful at every level of football. The higher the level (youth to professional), the more capable the coach and coaching staff needs to be to get the most out of their talent to compete. The same is true with software systems. As systems become more complex, there are more requirements for discipline, organization, depth of understanding of key concepts, experience, and attention to detail by the technical leadership.

Building a high-performing team that can successfully design and create today's modern complex systems (while maintaining conceptual integrity of design and sustainable agility) requires an experienced, qualified leader who can both design complex systems as well as lead and inspire the team. In other words, you need a head coach. Without this, you will have chaos.

Chief Engineer

The missing ingredient in many organizations is the role of what we call a chief engineer. Organizations often have people managing the projects and the people, but they do not have anyone managing the technical complexity of the projects. Suppose you are building an airplane or space satellite. In that case, you can rest assured that there is an individual who has oversight and responsibility for the system's technical success and readiness. This individual is actively working with the other engineers on a daily basis to make tactical and strategic decisions. This role is glaringly missing in our development organizations. Instead, we often have fragmented accountability via roles like architect, quality assurance, project manager, development team manager, etc. Who is responsible for functional quality? Who is responsible for the quality of the design? Who is responsible for application performance and security? When we have shared accountability for technical success and readiness, we have no accountability. Software development seems to be the only engineering discipline that does not have this chief engineer role. We need to fix this.

Responsibilities of a Chief Engineer

The problem of unmanaged technical complexity can destroy a software system over time. Failure to manage complexity becomes most apparent when there is a call for a rewrite of the software. When this occurs, it is usually a result of not having someone accountable for the quality of the system and how it is developed. This is why accountability for the technical success and execution of a software system should fall on the shoulders of a single individual – the chief engineer.

Being accountable for the technical success and execution means the chief engineer has many responsibilities, and one of them is *not* to be the best coder. A chief engineer needs to be a competent coder, but not necessarily the best coder. Their overall responsibility is to make everyone on their team more productive and ensure the short-term and long-term success of their software system. We can break this responsibility into eight key areas:

- Maintaining the big picture

- Maintaining conceptual integrity

- Seeing around corners

- Coaching and mentoring

- Building trusted relationships

- Being a proactive communicator

- Ensuring adequate testing

- Achieving technical success of the system

Maintaining the Big Picture

Keeping the big picture in mind is one of the key gaps filled by a chief engineer. It is very easy when working on projects to only think about solutions to the current problem. Someone needs to ensure that the solutions to the current problems also move the product toward its end goals.

In order to be effective, the chief engineer needs to start early on a project and stay with it through the lifecycle. It is very hard to come into an existing project and provide this level of leadership. This is why many architect roles in organizations are not as effective in this role. Once they do an architectural design, they disengage from the execution efforts.

The chief engineer needs to set the overall design for a system early on. This complete end system design might not be realized for years. The chief engineer must consider every change against the goal of achieving the end design. This is where having that design in place is so important. Without knowing where the system needs to go, making decisions along the way would be almost impossible.

The chief engineer is the person called upon to make sure the team is prepared for the technical challenges they will face. This is a tough job, but someone must own this responsibility to avoid chaos and software entropy.

Maintaining Conceptual Integrity

Many organizations federate technical decision-making. Each project, or each team, or each developer makes the technical decisions as they see fit. Sometimes they make conscious decisions to "build the plane while we fly it." The term "refactoring" is used in place of what is really happening: rework. Unless it is the very rare team of highly trained and experienced engineers, the result will be what you would expect: a system that appears to have been designed by many developers. The system will have no cohesion, it will be unmaintainable, forward progress eventually halts, and the calls for a "big rewrite" will be louder and more frequent.

The title "chief engineer" implies looking out for and caring for the technical aspect of a system. A large part of this responsibility is making sure that the system's implementation matches the design. Maintaining conceptual integrity is the most important thing a chief engineer will do. Technology misses are not as devastating as allowing the design of a system to rot. A chief engineer must remain diligent and active in nurturing and maintaining the quality and integrity of the system's design. The opposite of diligence and nurturing is leaving outcomes to chance, which will inevitably lead to chaos and software entropy.

Maintaining conceptual integrity involves making sure the proper critical thinking and design happen before changes are made and confirmed. This starts with ensuring that every developer does some detailed design whenever there are changes or modifications to the interfaces and interactions between various parts of the system. Any possibility for a violation of the information hiding principle must be considered and evaluated.

Individual developers should not be making architectural changes (changes to interfaces, adding components, etc.) without the involvement and blessing of the chief engineer. A building architect or general contractor would never allow skilled craftsmen to change the design of a building on their own.

Technical decisions can be as small as structuring a line of code to as big as structuring an entire workflow in the system. These decisions matter. Judgment errors can be caught during a code review, but it is better if they don't get made in the first place. As we have discussed, many problems are due to under-skilled staff and these errors in judgment. Gerald Weinberg has a great quote that captures this challenge:

No matter what they tell you, it is always a people problem.

—Gerald Weinberg

Finally, the chief engineer must perform code reviews of every change prior to accepting these changes into the main branch of code (or delegate this to someone of equal skill). Rather than just focusing on defects, this must involve evaluating the changes against the established design patterns and principles, best practices, and architecture design and constraints.

Seeing Around Corners

Chief engineers need to be looking around corners. In other words, anticipating something without actually seeing it, like coming to an intersection where you can't see crossing traffic and instinctively expect a vehicle to be coming from the left or right. This ability and skill manifests itself in two areas: (1) anticipating challenges and risk and (2) understanding the technology landscape and trajectory.

Our individual experience is something we often take for granted. There are specific problems and challenges we can anticipate without even thinking. Maybe it was some issue you encountered a few years ago or something you read about. When you are a chief engineer, you must share these insights with your team rather than assume they anticipate the same challenges. When working with a team of less experienced people, they will not have seen and experienced the variety of scenarios you have. One of the challenges with this is that you are likely surrounded by some bright (albeit young and relatively inexperienced) developers. Anticipating challenges and risks is less about intelligence and more about experiences. If you assume they will make good decisions because they are smart, you will be surprised when they come back and show you something that leaves you scratching your head.

The other aspect of seeing around corners is managing the technology landscape. A software platform must continue to evolve, and it needs to evolve within the industry. Being left entirely out of a new technology wave, or betting on the wrong wave, can have bad consequences for a platform. Chief engineers must stay up on technology trends, especially as it relates to the product they are supporting. The good news is there is lots of content out there. Following trends is possible because of the wealth of sources we have at our disposal.

Staying up with technology is not without challenges. First, you need to decide where to focus. Second, you need to find the time to keep up with the technology you chose to focus on. Both of these challenges must be solved. Staying up on industry trends is essential. Since you only have a limited amount of time, you must focus on the right sources. We recommend three investments. First, spend time with like-minded technology leaders. They will be looking at industry trends, too. You can benefit from their filter. Second, follow the trends of the platform you are running. If you are running on a Microsoft platform, follow the leaders in that space. Third, look at the overall industry trends. Where do you think the industry will be in five years? Try to look around the next corner. Some companies, like ThoughtWorks, do a good job of keeping their finger on the pulse of trends and periodically publish their opinions.[1]

If betting on the wrong technology or the wrong wave can be a problem, so can always focusing on new technologies. One of the biggest risks to any software product is the desire to always move to something newer. Sometimes the biggest value a chief engineer provides is keeping a project on existing technology. Likely, the existing platform is fine. Skipping a wave may be the better decision. Technology stacks and frameworks alone will not solve the challenge of managing complexity.

Coaching and Mentoring

Another major responsibility is coaching and mentoring the team. Chief engineers can't spend all of their time correcting poor decisions. Technical decisions are made by the software developers as they build the product. Because of the importance of these mini decisions, it is important that the software developers are trained to make sound decisions.

Coaching and mentoring will naturally happen during code reviews and other opportunities for the chief engineer to provide feedback. Each of these instances represents growth opportunities for the team members. The growth process can be enhanced by creating dedicated space for conversations outside of the normal daily rituals. The chief engineer could find time each month to spend an hour with each individual. This time can be used in a variety of ways: (1) pick a problem they are working on and walk through the thought process of the individual and the chief engineer, (2) find an interesting article and discuss pros and cons, (3) incrementally work though a technical book and discuss. The chief engineer can use these opportunities to share their thoughts and "war stories" from previous experiences.

Building Trusted Relationships

As the leader of the product development team, a chief engineer will need to interact with a variety of stakeholders outside of their team. Keeping these relationships healthy is critical not just for the leader but for the team as well.

---

[1]www.thoughtworks.com/radar

Things will progress much smoother when the chief engineer and stakeholders have a relationship built on respect and trust. The absence of this trust is never more apparent than when problems and challenges inevitably arise that threaten the goals and objectives of the stakeholders. With strong relationships in place, these challenges can be faced head-on with open and honest communication. Without trust, they may degrade into finger-pointing and blame-shifting.

Being a Proactive Communicator

A key to building trusted relationships is to be effective and proactive with communication. The hardest skill for many in our industry is the ability to communicate. Still, without the ability to communicate decisions and information to the team, all the other skills of a chief engineer will be less effective.

Proactive communication relates to staying ahead on communication and sharing information as early as possible. For example, suppose the chief engineer feels the target release date might be in jeopardy. This insight needs to be shared with stakeholders. Revealing this as soon as possible provides everyone with the most options to react to this information and develop strategies to mitigate.

A competent chief engineer is never afraid to share news and information they know some will consider as bad news. This also sends the right signals to your development team that they should be surfacing issues sooner rather than later, when options to address them will be more limited.

Ensuring Adequate Testing

Developing strategies for testing is another area where experience matters. Along with creating processes to analyze what tests should be developed, it is also necessary to anticipate areas of the system that might be at higher risk for defects. The chief engineer must guide the developers so that they can benefit from the experience and insight they have.

Much like sharing wisdom and experience when seeing around corners, the chief engineer must assume that these bright developers will not understand the potential complexities and errors that might exist. With few exceptions, most developers will be biased toward testing success paths within their code and assume that issues related to integration with other parts of the system will be rare. The chief engineer must continue to re-enforce the idea that the purpose of testing is to find defects, not prove the software is working.

Achieving Technical Success of the System

Finally, the chief engineer is responsible for, and should be held accountable for, the system's overall technical success. In addition to the responsibilities that have already been covered, several other areas related to technical success should fall under the responsibility of the chief engineer. These tend to be the most common accountabilities that are not adequately owned by a single individual.

- Execution Performance: This refers to whether the system has adequate execution performance and provides the ability to scale as necessary.

- Quality: This involves the testing strategy and ensuring that the proper level of code, security, and deployment testing is taking place. One might argue that other departments should be accountable for these items. The chief engineer is responsible for the team making the decisions that impact these aspects of quality. That is why the responsibility should be theirs and theirs alone.

- Project Execution: This refers to everything about the execution of the project. It involves ensuring the project kicks off efficiently, technical spikes are performed as necessary, and the team has everything they need to keep daily and weekly rituals productive and efficient. It also involves risk identification and communication.

Summary

When many organizations think of technical leadership, they are thinking of the best coder or the best manager. When they come upon a hot-shot coder, they promote them to a "leadership" position, which just means they need to compensate for issues created by other, less-capable members of their team. If they have some management skills, they might promote them to a management position where they are more focused on budgetary or personnel problems. The problem with these scenarios is that there is a gaping hole where an effective chief engineer is required. Someone must assume responsibility for the conceptual integrity of the design, the quality of the software, and the processes to be followed. Software development teams need a head coach who understands the technical details, keeps the big picture in mind, and has a game plan for crossing the finish line, all while not leaving anything to chance. They need a chief engineer.

Key Takeaways

- **It is critical to have someone that has and maintains the "big picture" on systems and projects**. This person is like a head coach.

- **A competent chief engineer is not necessarily your best coder**.

- **If everyone is accountable, no one is accountable**. Accountability should be centered on the chief engineer.

- **A chief engineer has many responsibilities** that should be clearly defined:

  - Maintaining the big picture

  - Maintaining conceptual integrity

  - Seeing around corners

  - Coaching and mentoring

  - Building trusted relationships

  - Being a proactive communicator

  - Ensuring adequate testing

  - Achieving the technical success of the project

CHAPTER 8

Bringing It All Together – Creating an Action Plan

Introduction

We have certainly thrown a lot at you by this point. You might be feeling overwhelmed by everything you need to do to transform your team and organization. It is important to understand that transforming a team and a culture is a process, not an event. As the saying goes, Rome was not built in a day. We have been involved in software development as far back as the late 1980s and 1990s, and this book is based upon that experience. We look at it very much like a continuing journey of discovery and growth. It's not as if we woke up one day and implemented all of the practices we have discussed. It happened over time, and there were some bumps along the road as we learned what was valuable and what was not. While we hope this book will help you avoid some of the red herrings we followed and wrong turns we might have made, it is important for you to realize this will be a journey for you as well. The question is, "Where should your journey start?" The goal of this chapter is to help you with these decisions.

What It Will Mean for Software Development to Be an Engineering Discipline

To start, it is helpful to develop a mental model of what it will look like when software development is practiced like other engineering disciplines. The world of software has a long history of relying on virtuoso performance and/or death marches to achieve success, even when dealing with complex systems that are not necessarily novel or innovative. This problem has become even more challenging as the complexity of the problems we

© Doug Durham and Chad Michel 2021
D. Durham and C. Michel, *Lean Software Systems Engineering for Developers*,
https://doi.org/10.1007/978-1-4842-6933-6_8

are trying to solve with software continues to grow and the near-constant pressure we are under to deliver the next feature and rapidly provide innovative solutions.

In contrast, other engineering disciplines are guided by sufficiently broad and accepted knowledge, patterns, and practices that have become established and widely known. Solutions to common problems are shared in a way that they can be reused to solve similar problems. This collective knowledge and the ability to effectively apply it allow the average engineer to successfully solve complex problems routinely and predictably. The need for exceptional engineers and talent is necessary only for those new problems that require innovation. This should be the ideal we are striving to achieve in software development.

The whole purpose of this book is to help software developers and development teams transform into an organization where they are not dependent on rock star performers and where a team of software developers can solve complex problems successfully, routinely, and predictably. A big benefit and key metric of this progress will be a significant reduction in the errors in judgment made by these development teams.

Starting Your Transformation

In this book, we have outlined a set of patterns and practices to demonstrate the breadth and depth required to create an engineering practice where these predictable outcomes become the norm. In Tables 8-1 to 8-5, we have summarized the key outcomes and the related patterns and practices for the themes that we covered in Chapters 2–6. Table 8-6 highlights the practices and outcomes for establishing the chief engineer role we discussed in Chapter 7.

Table 8-1. *Ensure shared understanding across the development team and stakeholders*

Practices	Desired Outcomes
Leverage lean approaches to backlog development	Increased shared understanding of requirements and business domain
Decompose and estimate stories to reduce uncertainty	Early identification of relevant information known to some but not known to all
	Early revelation of hidden assumptions and requirements that would surface later in development

Table 8-2. *Validation of user experience early and often*

Practices	Desired Outcomes
Reduce uncertainty with user interface spikes	Earlier access to user feedback and validation
Prioritize UI design and development to reduce rework	Reduction in project risk related to the volatility of the presentation layer
Use testable requirements to define robust and rigorous acceptance criteria	Increased likelihood that solution that is developed meets the needs of the intended customers

Table 8-3. *Software design that ages well*

Practices	Desired Outcomes
Increase strategic development	Avoided software decay and increased design stamina
Understand the principle of Information Hiding	Created a system that adapts to change and is more testable
Design and decompose systems based on encapsulating change	Maintained development velocity throughout the lifecycle of the system
Understand the nature of modern service-based systems	
Reduce the cognitive load of developers	
Actively manage the level of coupling within the system	

Table 8-4. *Developers "falling into the pit of success"*

Practices	Desired Outcomes
Ensure requirements and acceptance criteria are understood	Train junior developers
UI Design artifacts exist before development and are understood	Reduce errors in judgment
Consistent design identity	Reduce rework
Verify the design	
Testability	
Maker schedule	
Mentor relationship	
Establish clear developer expectations	

***Table 8-5.** Institutionalized quality*

Practices	Desired Outcomes
Establish quality accountability down to the developer	A culture where quality is everyone's concern
Layer quality practices to achieve industry-leading quality	Reduced rework
	Reduced need for "stabilization" at the end of release cycles
	Improved customer satisfaction

***Table 8-6.** Establishing a chief engineer role*

Practices	Desired Outcomes
Define the chief engineer role and model it after a coach	Increased productivity and consistency of the development team
Place accountability for the technical success of a project on the chief engineer	Broad adoption of best practices
	More predictable outcomes

Understanding the Maturity of Your Team

Before we build a plan for transformation, it can be valuable and insightful to better understand where your team currently stands and how they measure up. Everyone's journey will differ based upon their strengths and weaknesses. An assessment of your team or organization is the easiest way to gain visibility into their current state. Now that you have been exposed to what it means to develop software in a systematic, disciplined, and quantifiable way, you will have the proper perspective to assess your team or organization to compare against what we have covered. The results of your assessment will provide insights into areas where outcomes have a higher likelihood of being "left to chance" and/or where errors in judgment will most likely occur.

We have used the following assessment within several organizations, and we provide it here for you to use as a starting point for doing your own assessment. You should feel free to modify this and add other questions you feel are relevant to gain this understanding.

Lightweight Organizational Maturity Assessment

When we assess an organization, we ask people to answer the following questions using a scale of 1 to 10, with 1 meaning "Poor or Low" and 10 meaning "Solid or High." The assessment is divided into four areas.

Leadership Roles

- How effective is the technical leadership in your organization?

Managing Requirements Complexity

- How effective is your organization in creating a shared understanding of software requirements?

- How effective is your organization in decomposing requirements to reduce uncertainty?

- Does your team create UI designs in multiple stages (screen flow, wireframe, mockup)?

- Does your team create UI designs before work is assigned in sprints?

Solution Complexity

- How effective and valuable is your estimation process?

- How well does your organization design systems that age well?

- How effective is your organization in creating and maintaining loosely coupled/highly cohesive systems?

- How well do your systems respond to the need to implement new and changing requirements?

- How well does your organization protect and maintain the conceptual integrity of your designs?

- How devoted is your organization to always being "green" (i.e., constantly maintaining a working build and passing tests)?

- How well does your team manage quality?

- How well does your team leverage automated testing?

- How well does your team leverage code reviews?

Operational Effectiveness

- How effective are your project management processes?

- How maintainable are your software systems?

- How easy is it for you to comprehend your software systems when you need to make changes or add features?

- How productive does your calendar/schedule allow you to be?

- How easy is it for you, as a developer, to go through a code/build/debug/test cycle?

- How effective are your sprint cycles and rituals?

- How effective is your team in hitting deadlines and budget goals?

- How effective are your continuous integration automation workflows?

- How effective is your logging?

- How well does your organization collect and track development metrics?

The results of this survey can help inform your priorities as you review the following high-level actions that should be considered for your transformation plan. You can also periodically use the assessment to determine progress toward your plan. Your ultimate goal should be to achieve scores of 8–10 in all of the questions.

The Steps Toward Transformation

As we discussed, it has been helpful for us to think about the transformation of teams as a series of steps. These steps will allow you to focus on key, discrete, "bite-sized" areas and not feel like you have to "eat the whole elephant at one time." The reality is that our own development culture has evolved as a result of a series of these discrete steps over time.

The order in which we are discussing these steps represents the default order we would recommend starting with. Because these represent actions that are fairly distinct from one another, it is possible to tackle more than one at a time. Just realize that many of these steps will take significant time and energy to advocate, educate, and nurture to successful adoption. It is also important to note that these steps are continuous. You can't simply implement and be done. Each one requires continual monitoring, enhancement, nurturing. Software development, like other forms of engineering, is not static. Without constant attention and tuning, it will degrade into chaos like any other system.

Secure Your Platform

We don't discuss security in this book, but it goes without saying that you have a responsibility to ensure your application platform is secure before you tackle any of the following steps. It is likely that you are already taking steps to understand this risk and what is required to have a secure development lifecycle. If not, there are some excellent resources available online from organizations like the Open Web Application Security Project (OWASP) Foundation.[1] They are maybe best known for their "OWASP Top 10,"[2] a list of what they consider the current top ten most critical security risks in web applications. They have also developed a means of assessing an organization's security maturity through their "Software Assurance Maturity Model,"[3] also known as "OWASP SAMM."

Minimize Uncertainty

Utilize tools discussed throughout the book that are designed to reveal requirements and hidden assumptions. Validate the user experience early, before doing development work to minimize code changes. Leverage concepts like the "Cone of Uncertainty"[4] to educate all stakeholders and developers on the nature of estimation at various stages and the importance of managing this uncertainty to hit timelines and budget targets.

---

[1] https://owasp.org
[2] https://owasp.org/www-project-top-ten/
[3] https://owasp.org/www-project-samm/
[4] www.construx.com/books/the-cone-of-uncertainty/

Automate Your Builds

Replace manual build operations with modern tools that automate the build and deployment tasks, and trigger builds based upon events within the codebase. This step will improve developer productivity and reduce the chance for human error.

Protect Your Developer Time

Recognize the reality of the need for developers to have large, uninterrupted blocks of time to be productive. Modify recurring meetings to not fall in the middle of these big blocks of productive time. There have been several tools and apps that have been developed to help with time management. Consider an investment in some tools that enable you to track how much productive time your development team is really getting. Companies like Microsoft are even building analysis tools[5] into their cloud office platforms that provide amazing insights into how we are spending our time.

Maintain Conceptual Integrity

Adopt and establish a consistent software architecture methodology based upon "design for change." Close the gap between architects and developers so that they can regularly interact. Ensure architects are actively involved in the education and enforcement of architecture patterns and principles, down to the individual module interface designs. Use a pull request model to allow technical leaders to code review *all* changes to detect architecture principles violations, and ensure conceptual integrity is maintained down to a code level.

Improve Your Productivity by Improving Quality

Establish metrics for tracking defect detection rates and set a target of 95% defect detection. Combine this with the adoption of a variety of software quality best practices that will help achieve that target.

---

[5]www.microsoft.com/en-us/microsoft-365/business/myanalytics-personal-analytics

Reduce Rework

Establish metrics for tracking the amount of effort the development team spends on rework. Use this data to establish and achieve targets of < 25% of effort going to rework. Analyze the rework data to understand the sources and root causes of rework so that effective action can be taken to address the causes.

Improve Predictability and Visibility of Results

Improve the frequency of hitting release timelines and projections by tracking the accuracy of estimations and implementing changes to improve the accuracy. Allow stakeholders to see progress against plans by leveraging earned value tracking, which should show actual value earned vs. effort and plan.

Achieving the Ultimate "-ility"… Funability

We've been in the software business for quite some time. We are now counting our experience in decades instead of years. That's a *long* time, especially in this relatively young industry. When you've been part of a profession for that long, it can be easy to forget what initially attracted you to it.

We bring this up because we believe that some fundamental aspects of our industry are missing, and they're causing us damage. Maybe not initially, but they're slowly hurting us over time.

And if we're hurting, our products suffer.

As with so many industries, we in the software development sector too often reduce our workforce to the lowest common denominator of function. In our industry, that means turning our workers into little more than robotic programmers who just pound out code all day.

Add that feature. Fix this bug. Death marches toward impossible deadlines. And all this to what end? A checkmark placed next to another hastily implemented new feature?

There is more to this, right? There is a way to bring some semblance of life to the desert of code --> test --> release --> fix --> test --> release, right?

Yes, there is! Of course, we are talking about fun.

But we aren't talking about video games, free meals, beanbag chairs, and indoor slides. While those can be fun, we believe that "fun" needs to go deeper. We're talking about finding true enjoyment in the work itself. Because if we find honest satisfaction in what we are creating, how we are tackling problems, and why we are changing something for the better, we can consider "fun" the curtain that – when pulled back – reveals a rarely achieved level of personal and professional fulfillment.

When we started our latest venture in 2010, we knew that we had to take a different approach to software development. Anybody can build out a fun workspace, but we learned from our past experiences that we needed to go beyond the creature comforts typically found in the startup world. We needed to identify the real, soul-feeding fuel that gets us out of bed every morning and drives us to get our best selves in front of the day's challenges.

To do this, we had to examine where pain points existed within our daily routines and get them out of the way so our developers could focus on projects and enjoy the journeys through them. But to find that seed of gratification, we had to remind ourselves why we originally chose this career.

As we thought back through the years (no old-age jokes, please), we came up with this list of motivations that informed and drove our initial passions for software development:

- Rapid return on our efforts

- Work on tough problems

- Build tools that people use

- Enrich our lives

- Build something innovative

- Impact lives of others

- Save money/create wealth

- Automate complex activities

These are what we wanted to pay attention to, make them the focus of our daily work. As we discussed in Chapter 6, we wanted an environment where *what we enjoy* outweighs *what we loathe.*

As we were thinking through all of this, we came up with a term that describes it: funability. We defined it as "the measure of how well our culture and processes enable us to realize the motivations that got us into the business in the first place." Since we have so many other "-ilities" in our work lives (scalability, maintainability, etc.), we felt this word made sense in a clever sort of way.

We often end our training courses with a discussion of what Funability can look like for a developer, and we thought it would be appropriate to end this book the same way. If you find yourself in an environment with turnover, you might focus on this topic as it can help create an engaged, self-actualized workforce that is less likely to be looking for the next thing.

What Contributes to Funability

As soon as we defined what we wanted, we had to figure out how we would keep it at the forefront of our culture and daily practices and keep our developers engaged in our culture, company, and software development processes. We came up with seven points that we felt best encompassed our philosophy of funability.

Frequent Delivery of Value to Customers

This comes from our agile-inspired development environment. Earlier in our careers, we were pushing out releases only two or three times a year. It was a slow build-up that, in many ways, was made slower by less-than-ideal practices. And when you build up that much code over that much time, it can create a lot of pain before it even makes it out the door. There was a lot to pull together. Through that, we found that if we can increase the frequency at which we deliver fresh features to customers, we not only increase their satisfaction but our own satisfaction too.

Being Part of a Team

Obvious, right? Maybe not so much in some environments. In the military, they have the term *esprit de corps*, a feeling of pride and a common loyalty among members of a group. We believe that with a spirit of mutual accountability among the team members, we can be freed up to run a very flat organization. There are no managers, only developers; the teams run themselves. And it's that kind of empowerment that deeply instills a feeling of ownership and personal achievement, which is tough to create in other ways.

Maintainability of Systems

Here's an aspect that is easier said than done. Building software that can be easily read, understood, and debugged is a big deal. And once it's done right, it will reap benefits for many versions down the road (if the initial principles are upheld). Making it easy for developers to jump right into a system and quickly understand the impact changes will have is quite valuable.

This robust base from which a system can grow and change gives team members that sense of "yeah, we're getting stuff done." And as we can all attest, that beats the alternative of spending what can seem like countless hours deciphering what others have done in the past.

Effective Management of Technical Debt

Ah, technical debt. It will always be with us, but we can limit its drag on our projects by first recognizing when choices may increase our technical debt. Typically (and at the most basic level), this means not implementing features the quickest way possible but taking the time necessary to understand the trade-offs that may lead to a less than optimal design (a.k.a. errors in judgment).

In the ideal case, we can find a path to avoid taking on the debt. But when this cannot be avoided, we need to acknowledge the risk and plan (e.g., via a new backlog item) for how we will deal with it down the road. Maybe the most important part of this is the conversation and the shared understanding by the team of the choices being made.

Consistent Quality of Product Releases

As previously discussed, back in the early 2000s, we developed and managed an ecommerce platform. Releases were done only a few times a year, and for good reason: we were on pins and needles the whole time. Would it work? What would break? How seriously would it break? How quickly could we fix it? It was a very stressful time that, to this day, still gives us anxiety by just thinking it about.

These past headaches are one of the driving reasons why we approach releases the way we do today. The importance of having smooth releases cannot be overstated, especially when you're updating mission-critical systems. Living in dread of release days does not make for healthy work environments.

Productivity and Efficiency of the Developers

One of the best things we can do for our developers is to reduce their distractions and "clear the road," so to speak. By doing this, we're giving them enough time to get into a problem and work it out. Allowing them to be constantly interrupted by numerous meetings or additional side-tasks just creates frustrations or, even worse, less-than-optimal solutions.

There are a variety of things we do that fall under the categories of productivity and efficiency: the role of project management, how we physically organize the office space, the structure of our teams, and the way we design the software itself.

Sound Software Design

We hope that by this point you understand that maintaining some sort of consistency in your conceptual system designs is key. Providing consistency across your entire platform is what makes flexibility possible within your team. When everything is designed and developed using the same philosophies and concepts, moving team members around to different projects becomes a lot less risky and inefficient.

For example, if a project requires a short burst of extra development muscle, we can augment a team with additional developers very quickly. Imagine an environment where the developers, without losing productivity, can float between different parts of a large system as the need for resources ebbs and flows. This kind of flexibility would be very desirable to an organization and has been a capability we have leveraged often. By keeping our methodologies consistent, it doesn't take much for the "new folks" to get up to speed on the project. They can get going very quickly.

Consistency also prioritizes simplicity over cleverness. Sometimes, a clever approach to a problem can be fun, but it often adds unnecessary (or accidental) complexity. This can act as a speed bump for someone needing to learn the code base and cause problems when new features are implemented. Our discipline in this area has also helped us scope projects for estimation. Nearly everything becomes more predictable when we stick to known and repeatable processes and patterns.

This is the bedrock of our culture and is something we've been doing since Day One. We're not dogmatic about much, but this one may be the closest thing to religious adherence we have.

Now What?

We wrote this book to share our experiences and journey as we strive to achieve the ultimate goal of successfully solving complex problems in a repeatable, predictable way and doing it while having fun. We hope that reading this book will help you with your own journey to achieve the same. Our industry has enormous possibilities for positive contributions to society and improving the lives and well-being of countless people. We need to change the way we tackle these problems if we are going to realize our potential.

Key Takeaways

- **It is reasonable to expect software development to have the same discipline and predictable outcomes as other areas of engineering.**

- **It is important to have a thoughtful approach to transforming your team.**

    - Everyone is a little different.

    - There needs to be a plan.

    - The plan should not be to tackle everything at once.

- **Software development should be "fun."**

- Above all else, **"leave nothing to chance."**

Index

A

Abstract mental model, 40
Architectural designs, 138
Assumptions, 42, 46, 132
Automated/manual tests, 50, 80, 138, 162

B

Back-end programming environments, 55
Basis testing, 140, 142
Boundary checking, 140
Boundary checking analysis, 142
Building systems, 73
    experiences, 74, 75
    reality check, 73, 74
Business goals, 152

C

Can-do attitude, 128
Chief engineer, 171
    big picture, 172
    coaching and mentoring, 175
    conceptual integrity, 172, 173
    proactive communicator, 176
    relationships, 176
    responsibility, 171
    seeing around corners, 174
    technical success, 177
    testing, 176

Code reviews, 147, 162, 163
Code smell, 16
Cohesion, 99, 100, 164, 172
Conceptual integrity, 137, 172, 173
Coupling, 18, 89, 97, 99, 100

D

Database framework, 122
Data flow testing, 140, 142
Data Transfer Object (DTO), 68, 138
Decomposing systems, 100, 101
Defect detection rate, 154, 155
Design artifacts, 129, 135, 138, 161
Design constraints, 131
Design identity, 136, 138
Designing systems
    change, 108
    choose methodology, 114, 115
    complexity, 113, 114
    comprehend, 110–112
    modern applications/business
        agility, 112, 113
Design Stamina Hypothesis, 108, 109, 152
Developers, 120
    objectives, 128
    expectations, 145, 161
Developers changing technologies, 125
Developers upgrading
    technologies, 125

© Doug Durham and Chad Michel 2021
D. Durham and C. Michel, *Lean Software Systems Engineering for Developers*,
https://doi.org/10.1007/978-1-4842-6933-6

U, V

W, X, Y, Z

Printed in the United States
by Baker & Taylor Publisher Services

Printed in the United States
by Baker & Taylor Publisher Services